OFFICIAL SQA PAST PAPERS

WITH ANSWERS

HIGHER

ENGLISH
2008-2012

D0320648

✕SQA

BrightRED
PUBLISHING

First exam published in 2008.
Published by Bright Red Publishing Ltd, 6 Stafford Street, Edinburgh EH3 7AU
tel: 0131 220 5804 fax: 0131 220 6710 info@brightredpublishing.co.uk www.brightredpublishing.co.uk

ISBN 978-1-84948-286-8

A CIP Catalogue record for this book is available from the British Library.

Bright Red Publishing is grateful to the copyright holders, as credited on the final page of the Question Section, for permission to use their material.
Every effort has been made to trace the copyright holders and to obtain their permission for the use of copyright material.
Bright Red Publishing will be happy to receive information allowing us to rectify any error or omission in future editions.

HIGHER

2008

[BLANK PAGE]

X115/301

NATIONAL
QUALIFICATIONS
2008

THURSDAY, 15 MAY
9.00 AM – 10.30 AM

ENGLISH
HIGHER
~~Close Reading~~ Text
Essay.

There are TWO passages and questions.

Read the passages carefully and then answer all the questions, which are printed in a separate booklet.

You should read the passages to:

understand what the writers are saying about the countryside and those who campaign to protect it (**Understanding–U**);

analyse their choices of language, imagery and structures to recognise how they convey their points of view and contribute to the impact of the passage (**Analysis–A**);

evaluate how effectively they have achieved their purpose (**Evaluation–E**).

PASSAGE 1

In this extract from his book "Shades of Green", David Sinclair looks at attitudes to the countryside and discusses to what extent it is part of "our heritage".

Choose   **RURAL MANIA**   and explain.

The "countryside debate" has rarely been out of the news in Britain in recent years. Reading the newspapers, watching television, listening to the radio, entering a bookshop, one could be forgiven for thinking that we still live in small peasant communities dependent upon the minutest shift in agricultural policy. Sometimes it
5 has seemed almost as if we were still in the early nineteenth century when we relied on the countryside to survive, so extensive have been the debates, so fierce the passions aroused.

One faction has cried constantly that the countryside is in mortal danger from greedy developers whose only motive is profit; another has kept on roaring that
10 farmers are killing every wild thing in sight and threatening the very soil on which we stand through overuse of machinery and chemicals; still another has been continually heard ululating over a decline in the bird population, or the loss of hedgerows, or the disappearance of marshland, or the appearance of coniferous forest.

15 Then there is the proliferation of action groups dedicated to stopping construction of roads, airports, railway lines, factories, shopping centres and houses in rural areas, while multifarious organisations have become accustomed to expending their time and energies in monitoring and reporting on the state of grassland, water, trees, moorlands, uplands, lowlands, birds' eggs, wildflowers, badgers, historical sites and
20 countless other aspects of the landscape and its inhabitants.

It might be thought—indeed, it is widely assumed—that it must be good for the countryside to be returned to the central position it enjoyed in British life long ago. Yet there is a particularly worrying aspect of the new rural mania that suggests it might finally do the countryside more harm than good.

25 This is the identification, in the current clamour, of the countryside in general and the landscape in particular with the past—the insistence on the part of those who claim to have the best intentions of ruralism at heart that their aim is to protect what they glibly refer to as "our heritage". This wildly over-used term is seriously misleading, not least because nobody appears ever to have asked what it means.

30 The assumption is that the landscape is our living link with our history, the visible expression of our British roots, and that if we allow it to change ("to be destroyed", the conservationists would say), the link is broken forever. This view is palpably nonsensical. Our national identity is not defined by the landscape against which we carry on our lives. There is, in fact, no single thread that can be identified as our
35 rural heritage or tradition. Rather there is a bewildering array of different influences that have combined haphazardly through the centuries as successive invaders and immigrants and, later, successive generations, have reconstructed the landscape according to their own needs and ideas. What the conservationists seek to preserve is simply the landscape *as it is now*, in its incarnation of the early twenty-
40 first century. Far from affirming history, this approach actually denies it, for it would remove the continuous change without which history does not exist.

Where, for example, does the "traditional" landscape begin and end? If we take the period when the British Isles were born, nearly 8,000 years ago, we discover that the

conifers so hated by the conservationists today were one of the most important
45　features of the scenery; the "English" oak and the much-loved elm were later
immigrants from the warmer south. As for fauna, our "traditional" species included
reindeer, rhinoceros, bison, hippopotamus and elephant. But where are they now?

Perhaps we should do better in the search for our heritage to consider what the
countryside looked like when man first appeared in what we think of as Britain.
50　That would take us back 35,000 years, to the emergence of our ancestor *Homo
sapiens*, who found himself in an Arctic landscape of ice and tundra. The remnants
of that traditional scene can be found only in the highest mountains of Scotland; the
rest of Britain has changed beyond recognition.

Obviously, then, we must look at more recent times if we are to discover identifiable
55　traditional elements in the landscape we now see about us. Yet if we do that, further
difficulties emerge. The retreat of the last glaciation almost 11,000 years ago was
accompanied by a relatively rapid warming of the climate, which gradually
converted the open Arctic tundra into dense forest. This presented a serious
challenge to Stone Age man, who began to find that the grazing animals, which he
60　hunted for food, were disappearing as their habitat retreated before the encroaching
trees. In order to survive, he was forced to turn increasingly from hunting to
farming, with the dramatic effects on flora and fauna that remain familiar to us
today. As the quality of prehistoric tools improved, some stretches of forest were
felled to provide grazing for domesticated animals, while grasses and cereals were
65　deliberately encouraged because of their usefulness to man. Even the shape of the
countryside was changed as mining began to cut into hillsides, and in some places
soil deterioration set in as the growing populations demanded perhaps the earliest
form of intensive farming. In other words, the chief influence on the landscape of
these islands was not nature but mankind.

PASSAGE 2

*In the second passage, the journalist Richard Morrison responds to criticism of a Government
plan to allow a million new houses to be built in southeast England.*

PULLING UP THE DRAWBRIDGE

The English middle classes are rarely more hypocritical than when waxing
indignant about "the threat to the countryside". What anguishes them usually
turns out to be the threat to their own pleasure or to the value of their property.
And I write those sentences with the heavy heart of a class traitor, for I am a
5　middle-class, middle-aged property owner who has smugly watched his own house
soar in value as more and more young househunters desperately chase fewer and
fewer properties. I am inordinately proud of my view across the green belt (from
an upstairs window admittedly, because of the motorway flyover in between). And
I intend to spend the weekend rambling across the rural England I have loved since
10　boyhood.

The most cherished credo of the English middle classes is that the verdant hills
and dales of the Home Counties should remain forever sacrosanct, and that the
Government's "Stalinist" decision to impose a million extra houses on southeast
England is the most hideous threat to our way of life since the Luftwaffe made its
15　energetic contribution to British town and country planning in 1940. Thousands

of green acres will be choked by concrete, as rapacious housebuilders devour whole landscapes. England's cherished green belts—the 14 great rings of protected fields that have stopped our major cities from sprawling outward for more than half a century—will be swept away.

20 Yet if you sweep away the apoplectic froth and the self-interested posturing and look at the reality, the "threat to the countryside" recedes dramatically. Yes, we do occupy a crowded little island. But what makes it seem crowded is that 98 per cent of us live on 7 per cent of the land. Britain is still overwhelmingly green. Just 11 per cent of our nation is classified as urban.

25 Moreover, planners reckon that as much as a quarter of the green belt around London is wasteland, largely devoid of landscape beauty. So why not use it to relieve the intolerable pressure on affordable housing in the capital? Because that would contravene the long-held myth that green belts are vital "lungs" for cities. Well, lungs they might be. But they benefit chiefly those who live in nice houses 30 inside the green belts (not least by keeping their property values sky-high); and then those who live in nice houses in the leafy outer suburbs; and not at all the people who need the fresh air most: those on inner-city estates.

The green-belt protectionists claim to be saving unspoilt countryside from the rampant advance of bulldozers. Exactly what unspoilt countryside do they imagine 35 they are saving? Primordial forest, unchanged since Boadicea thrashed the Romans? Hogwash. The English have been making and remaking their landscape for millennia to suit the needs of each passing generation.

These protectionists are fond of deriding any housebuilding targets set by the Government as monstrous, Soviet-style diktats. Good grief, what on earth do they 40 imagine that the planning laws protecting green belts and agricultural land are, if not Government interventions that have had a huge, and often disastrous, impact not just on the property market, but on employment, on transport, on public services and on economic growth?

And, of course, on homelessness. Every time a bunch of middle-class homeowners 45 fights off the "intrusion" of a new housing estate into their cherished landscape, they make it more difficult for the young and the poor to find somewhere to live in reasonable proximity to where they can find work. This is the 21st-century equivalent of pulling up the drawbridge after one's own family and friends are safely inside the castle.

[END OF TEXT]

X115/302

NATIONAL
QUALIFICATIONS
2008

THURSDAY, 15 MAY
9.00 AM – 10.30 AM

ENGLISH
HIGHER
Close Reading–Questions

Answer all questions. **Use your own words whenever possible and particularly when you are instructed to do so.**

50 marks are allocated to this paper.

A code letter (U, A, E) is used alongside each question to give some indication of the skills being assessed. The number of marks attached to each question will give some indication of the length of answer required.

Questions on Passage 1

Marks   *Code*

1. Read lines 1–7.

   Explain in your own words why the writer seems surprised that there is so much coverage of the "countryside debate". (line 1)   **2**   **U**

2. (*a*) Show how the word choice **and** sentence structure in lines 8–14 emphasise the strong feelings of those who feel the countryside is under threat.   **4**   **A**

   (*b*) Show how the writer's use of language in lines 15–20 conveys his disapproval of the "action groups".   **2**   **A**

3. Read lines 21–29.

   (*a*) By referring to specific words or phrases, show how lines 21–24 perform a linking function at this stage in the writer's argument.   **2**   **U**

   (*b*) Referring to lines 25–29, explain in your own words what the writer believes to be a "particularly worrying aspect of the new rural mania" (line 23).   **2**   **U**

4. "This view is palpably nonsensical." (lines 32–33)

   (*a*) Explain, using your own words as far as possible, what "this view" is. Refer to lines 30–32 in your answer.   **2**   **U**

   (*b*) Give in your own words **one** of the writer's reasons in lines 33–38 (". . . ideas.") for believing that the view is "palpably nonsensical".   **2**   **U**

   (*c*) Show how the writer's use of language in lines 38–41 reinforces his criticism of the conservationists' ideas.   **2**   **A**

5. Read lines 42–53.

   Give, in your own words as far as possible, any **three** reasons why it is difficult to define the "traditional" British landscape.   **3**   **U**

6. "This presented a serious challenge to Stone Age man . . ." (lines 58–59)

   (*a*) Explain in your own words what the "challenge" was. Refer to lines 54–61 (". . . trees.") in your answer.   **2**   **U**

   (*b*) Explain in your own words how Stone Age man responded to the challenge. Refer to lines 61–69 in your answer.   **2**   **U**

      (25)

Questions on Passage 2

Marks   Code

7. (*a*) By referring to lines 1–3, explain in your own words why the writer believes that the English middle classes are being "hypocritical".   2   **U**

   (*b*) Show how the writer's use of language in lines 4–10 creates a self-mocking tone.   2   **A**

8. Show how the writer's use of language in lines 11–19 emphasises the extreme nature of the English middle classes' view of the threat to the countryside.

   In your answer you should refer to specific language features such as: imagery, word choice, register . . .   4   **A**

9. Show how the writer's sentence structure **or** word choice in lines 20–24 emphasises his view that the threat to the countryside is much less serious than the English middle classes suggest.   2   **A**

10. (*a*) According to lines 25–27, why does the writer believe "a quarter of the green belt around London" should be used for housing?   2   **U**

    (*b*) How does the writer's use of language in lines 27 ("Because . . .") –32 cast doubt on the belief that green belts benefit everyone?   2   **A**

11. In lines 33–43 the writer criticises two further arguments put forward by the "green-belt protectionists".

    Choose **either** the argument discussed in lines 33–37 **or** the argument discussed in lines 38–43, and answer **both** of the following questions on the paragraph you have chosen.

    (*a*) Explain why, in the writer's opinion, the green-belt protectionists' argument is flawed.   2   **U**

    (*b*) How effective do you find the writer's use of language in conveying his attitude to their argument?   2   **A/E**

12. How effective do you find lines 44–49 as a conclusion to the writer's attack on the attitudes of "middle-class homeowners"?   2   **E**

                                                                                        (20)

Question on both Passages

13. In Passage 1 David Sinclair refers to the claims of conservationists as "palpably nonsensical" and in Passage 2 Richard Morrison states that their views are "hogwash". Which writer is more successful in convincing you that these conservationists' claims are seriously flawed?

    Justify your choice by referring to the **ideas and/or style** of **both passages**.   5   **E**

                                                                                        (5)

                                                                            Total (50)

[END OF QUESTION PAPER]

[BLANK PAGE]

X115/303

NATIONAL
QUALIFICATIONS
2008

THURSDAY, 15 MAY
10.50 AM – 12.20 PM

ENGLISH
HIGHER
Critical Essay

Answer **two** questions.

Each question must be taken from a different section.

Each question is worth 25 marks.

Answer TWO questions from this paper. Each question must be chosen from a different Section (A–E). You are not allowed to choose two questions from the same Section.

In all Sections you may use Scottish texts.

Write the number of each question in the margin of your answer booklet and begin each essay on a fresh page.

You should spend about 45 minutes on each essay.

The following will be assessed:

- the relevance of your essays to the questions you have chosen, and the extent to which you sustain an appropriate line of thought

- your knowledge and understanding of key elements, central concerns and significant details of the chosen texts, supported by detailed and relevant evidence

- your understanding, as appropriate to the questions chosen, of how relevant aspects of structure/style/language contribute to the meaning/effect/impact of the chosen texts, supported by detailed and relevant evidence

- your evaluation, as appropriate to the questions chosen, of the effectiveness of the chosen texts, supported by detailed and relevant evidence

- the quality of your written expression and the technical accuracy of your writing.

SECTION A—DRAMA

Answers to questions on drama should address relevantly the central concern(s)/theme(s) of the text and be supported by reference to appropriate dramatic techniques such as: conflict, characterisation, key scene(s), dialogue, climax, exposition, dénouement, structure, plot, setting, aspects of staging (such as lighting, music, stage set, stage directions . . .), soliloquy, monologue . . .

1. Choose a play in which a central character is heroic yet vulnerable.

   Show how the dramatist makes you aware of both qualities and discuss how they affect your response to the character's fate in the play as a whole.

2. Choose a play which explores the theme of love in difficult circumstances.

   Explain how the dramatist introduces the theme and discuss how in the course of the play he/she prepares you for the resolution of the drama.

3. Choose from a play a scene in which an important truth is revealed.

   Briefly explain what the important truth is and assess the significance of its revelation to your understanding of theme or character.

4. Choose a play in which a character has to exist in a hostile environment.

   Briefly describe the environment and discuss the extent to which it influences your response to the character's behaviour and to the outcome of the play.

SECTION B—PROSE

Prose Fiction

> *Answers to questions on prose fiction should address relevantly the central concern(s)/theme(s) of the text(s) and be supported by reference to appropriate techniques of prose fiction such as: characterisation, setting, key incident(s), narrative technique, symbolism, structure, climax, plot, atmosphere, dialogue, imagery . . .*

5. Choose a **novel** which explores the cruelty of human nature.

    Show how the writer explores this theme and discuss how its exploration enhances your appreciation of the novel as a whole.

6. Choose a **novel** in which a confrontation between two characters is of central importance in the text.

    Explain the circumstances of the confrontation and discuss its importance to your understanding of the novel as a whole.

7. Choose **two short stories** which you appreciated because of the surprising nature of their endings.

    Compare the techniques used in creating these surprising endings and discuss which ending you feel is more successful as a conclusion.

8. Choose a **novel** or **short story** which is set during a period of social or political change.

    Discuss how important the writer's evocation of the period is to your appreciation of the text as a whole.

Prose Non-fiction

> *Answers to questions on prose non-fiction should address relevantly the central concern(s)/theme(s) of the text and be supported by reference to appropriate techniques of prose non-fiction such as: ideas, use of evidence, selection of detail, point of view, stance, setting, anecdote, narrative voice, style, language, structure, organisation of material . . .*

9. Choose a **non-fiction text** which you consider inspiring or provocative.

    Explain how the writer's presentation of his/her subject has such an impact on you.

10. Choose a piece of **travel writing** which offers surprising or amusing insights into a particular country or culture.

    Explain briefly what you learn about the country or culture and in greater detail discuss the techniques the writer uses to surprise or amuse you.

11. Choose a **non-fiction text** in which you consider the writer's stance on a particular issue to be ambiguous.

    Show how the writer's presentation of this issue illustrates the ambiguity of her/his stance.

[Turn over

SECTION C—POETRY

Answers to questions on poetry should address relevantly the central concern(s)/theme(s) of the text(s) and be supported by reference to appropriate poetic techniques such as: imagery, verse form, structure, mood, tone, sound, rhythm, rhyme, characterisation, contrast, setting, symbolism, word choice . . .

12. Choose a poem which deals with conflict or danger or death.

Show how the poet creates an appropriate mood for the subject matter and go on to discuss how effectively she/he uses this mood to enhance your understanding of the central idea of the poem.

13. Choose a poem which is strongly linked to a specific location.

Show how the poet captures the essence of the location and exploits this to explore an important theme.

14. Choose **two** poems which explore human relationships.

By referring to both poems, discuss which you consider to be the more convincing portrayal of a relationship.

15. Choose a poem in which the speaker's personality is gradually revealed.

Show how, through the content and language of the poem, aspects of the character gradually emerge.

SECTION D—FILM AND TV DRAMA

> *Answers to questions on film and TV drama should address relevantly the central concern(s)/theme(s) of the text(s) and be supported by reference to appropriate techniques of film and TV drama such as: key sequence(s), characterisation, conflict, structure, plot, dialogue, editing/montage, sound/soundtrack, aspects of mise-en-scène (such as lighting, colour, use of camera, costume, props . . .), mood, setting, casting, exploitation of genre . . .*

16. Choose a **film** or **TV drama*** in which a particular sequence is crucial to your understanding of an important theme.

    By referring to the sequence and to the text as a whole, show why you consider the sequence to be so important to your understanding of the theme.

17. Choose a **film** or **TV drama*** which presents a life-affirming story.

    By referring to key elements of the text, show how the story has such an effect.

18. Choose a **film** or **TV drama*** in which intense feelings have tragic consequences.

    Show to what extent the film or programme makers' presentation of these feelings and their consequences is successful in engaging you with the text.

19. Choose a **film** or **TV drama*** in which a complex character is revealed.

    Show how the film or programme makers reveal the complexity and discuss to what extent this aspect of the character contributes to your response to the text.

*"TV drama" includes a single play, a series or a serial.

[Turn over

SECTION E—LANGUAGE

Answers to questions on language should address relevantly the central concern(s) of the language research/study and be supported by reference to appropriate language concepts such as: register, jargon, tone, vocabulary, word choice, technical terminology, presentation, illustration, accent, grammar, idiom, slang, dialect, structure, point of view, orthography, abbreviation . . .

20. Consider uses of language designed to interest you in a social or commercial or political campaign.

    Identify aspects of language which you feel are intended to influence you and evaluate their success in raising your awareness of the subject of the campaign.

21. Consider the spoken language of a clearly defined group of people.

    Identify features which differentiate this language from standard usage and assess the extent to which these features have useful functions within the group.

22. Consider the language of newspaper reporting on such subjects as fashion, celebrities, reality TV, soap stars. . .

    Identify some of the characteristics of this language and discuss to what extent it is effective in communicating with its target audience.

23. Consider the language (written and/or symbolic) associated with the use of e-mails or text messaging or instant messaging.

    Describe some of the conventions associated with any one of these and discuss to what extent these conventions lead to more effective communication.

[END OF QUESTION PAPER]

[BLANK PAGE]

X115/301

NATIONAL QUALIFICATIONS 2009	FRIDAY, 15 MAY 9.00 AM – 10.45 AM	ENGLISH HIGHER Close Reading—Text

There are TWO passages and questions.

Read the passages carefully and then answer all the questions, which are printed in a separate booklet.

You should read the passages to:

understand what the writers are saying about issues surrounding our use of natural resources (**Understanding–U**);

analyse their choices of language, imagery and structures to recognise how they convey their points of view and contribute to the impact of the passage (**Analysis–A**);

evaluate how effectively they have achieved their purpose (**Evaluation–E**).

PASSAGE 1

The first passage is from an article in The Telegraph *newspaper in January 2007. In it, Janet Daley responds to suggestions that we should limit our use of natural resources.*

A DOOMSDAY SCENARIO?

Is your journey really necessary? Who would have thought that, in the absence of world war and in the midst of unprecedented prosperity, politicians would be telling us not to travel? Just as working people have begun to enjoy the freedoms that the better-off have known for generations—the experience of other cultures, other
5 cuisines, other climates—they are threatened with having those liberating possibilities priced out of their reach.

And when I hear politicians—most of them comfortably off—trying to deny enlightenment and pleasure to "working class" people, I reach for my megaphone. Maybe Tommy Tattoo and his mates do use cheap flights to the sunshine as an
10 extension of their binge-drinking opportunities, but for thousands of people whose parents would never have ventured beyond Blackpool or Rothesay, air travel has been a social revelation.

So, before we all give the eco-lobby's anti-flying agenda the unconditional benefit of the doubt, can we just review their strategy as a whole?

15 Remember, it is not just air travel that the green tax lobby is trying to control: it is a restriction on any mobility. Clamping down on one form of movement, as the glib reformers have discovered, simply creates intolerable pressure on the others. Londoners, for example, had just become accustomed to the idea that they would have to pay an £8 congestion charge to drive into their own city when they
20 discovered that the fares on commuter rail and underground services had been hiked up with the intention of driving away customers from the public transport system—now grossly overcrowded as a result of people having been forced off the roads by the congestion charge.

The only solution—and I am just waiting for the politicians to recommend it
25 explicitly—is for none of us to go anywhere. Stay at home and save the planet. But that would be a craven retreat from all the social, professional and cultural interactions that unrestricted mobility makes possible—and which, since the Renaissance, have made great cities the centres of intellectual progress.

Even devising a way of making a living while never leaving your house would not
30 absolve you of your ecological guilt, because you'd still be making liberal use of the technology that has transformed domestic life. The working classes, having only discovered in the last generation or two the comforts of a tolerable degree of warmth and plentiful hot water, are now being told that these things must be rationed or prohibitively taxed.

35 Never mind that the universal presence of adequate heating has almost eliminated those perennial scourges of the poor—bronchitis and pneumonia—which once took the very young and the very old in huge numbers every winter. Never mind that the generous use of hot water and detergent, particularly when combined in a washing machine for the laundering of bed linen and clothing, has virtually eliminated the
40 infestations of body lice and fleas (which once carried plague) that used to be a commonplace feature of poverty. Never mind that the private car, the Green Public Enemy Number One, has given ordinary families freedom and flexibility that would have been inconceivable in previous generations.

If politicians are planning restrictions on these "polluting" aspects of private life, to
45　be enforced by a price mechanism, they had better accept that they will be
reconstructing a class divide that will drastically affect the quality of life of those on
the wrong side of it.

It is certainly possible that the premises advanced by environmental campaigners are
sound: that we are in mortal danger from global warming and that this is a result of
50　human activity. Yet when I listen to ecological warnings such as these, I am
reminded of a doomsday scenario from the past.

In his *Essay on the Principle of Population*, published in 1798, Thomas Malthus
demonstrated, in what appeared to be indisputable mathematical terms, that
population growth would exceed the limits of food supply by the middle of the 19th
55　century. Only plague, war or natural disaster would be capable of sufficiently
reducing the numbers of people to avert mass starvation within roughly 50 years.
This account of the world's inevitable fate (known as the "Malthusian catastrophe")
was as much part of accepted thinking among intellectuals then as are the
environmental lobby's warnings today.

60　Malthus, however, had made a critical conceptual mistake: he underestimated the
complexity of human behaviour. Population did not go on increasing at the same
rate; it responded to economic and social conditions. Moreover, he had discounted
the force of ingenuity in finding ways to increase food supply. In actual fact, the
introduction of intensive farming methods and the invention of pesticides
65　transformed what he had assumed would be the simple, fixed relation between
numbers of people and amount of resource. He had made what seemed to be a
sound prediction without allowing for the possibility that inventiveness and
innovation might alter the picture in unimaginable ways.

Warnings of catastrophe come and go. Whatever their validity, we cannot and
70　should not ask people to go back to a more restricted way of life. The restrictions
would not work anyway, because they are impracticable. If they were enforced, they
would be grotesquely unfair and socially divisive. If we really are facing an
environmental crisis, then we are going to have to innovate and engineer our way out
of it.

PASSAGE 2

Leo Hickman, writing in The Guardian *newspaper in May 2006, explores the ethics of leisure-related flights.*

IS IT OK TO FLY?

I am desperate for some good news about aviation and its environmental impact.
Please someone say that they got the figures wrong. I have always loved the
freedom and access flying brings—who doesn't?—but in recent years I have
descended into near-permanent depression about how to square this urge with the
5　role of at least trying to be a responsible citizen of the planet. Travel is one of life's
pleasures, but is my future—and, more importantly, that of my two young
daughters—really going to be one of abstinence from flying, or at best flying by
quota, as many environmentalists are now calling for?

I recently travelled to Geneva to attend the second "Aviation and Environment
10 Summit" in search of, if not answers, then at least a better indication of just how
damaging flying really is to the environment. (The irony was not lost that hundreds
of people had flown from around the world to attend.)

Speaker after speaker bemoaned how the public had somehow misunderstood the
aviation industry and had come to believe that aviation is a huge and
15 disproportionate polluter. Let's get this in perspective, said repeated speakers: this
is small fry compared with cars, factories, even homes. Why are we being singled
out, they cried? Why not, they said, chase after other industries that could easily
make efficiency savings instead of picking on an industry that gives so much to the
world, yet is currently so economically fragile?

20 But even in this self-interested arena a representative from the US Federal Aviation
Administration caused some sharp intakes of breath from the audience by showing
an extraordinary map of current flightpaths etched over one another on the world's
surface. The only places on Earth that are not scarred by routes are blocks of air
space over the central Pacific, the southern Atlantic and Antarctica.

25 It seems, therefore, that we who avidly consume cheap flights do indeed have to face
a choice. Do we continue to take our minibreaks, visit our second homes, holiday on
the other side of the world and partake of all the other forms of what the industry
describes as "non-essential" travel? Or do we start to ration this habit, even if
others elsewhere in the world quite understandably will be quick to take our place
30 on the plane? My view is that flying will simply have to become more expensive.
Only by becoming more expensive will ticket prices start to reflect more closely the
environmental impact of flying—the polluter should always pay, after all—and
therefore drive down demand. It's easy to forget how good we've had it in this
heady era of low-cost carriers—but surely the good times must end.

35 A remedy such as carbon-neutralising our flights is a nice, cuddly idea that on the
surface is a positive action to take, but planting trees in Thailand or handing out
eco-lightbulbs in Honduras is no substitute for getting planes out of the skies. It
also carries the risk that people will think "job done" and simply carry on flying
regardless.

[END OF TEXT]

X115/302

NATIONAL
QUALIFICATIONS
2009

FRIDAY, 15 MAY
9.00 AM – 10.45 AM

ENGLISH
HIGHER
Close Reading–Questions

Answer all questions. **Use your own words whenever possible and particularly when you are instructed to do so.**

50 marks are allocated to this paper.

A code letter (U, A, E) is used alongside each question to give some indication of the skills being assessed. The number of marks attached to each question will give some indication of the length of answer required.

Questions on Passage 1   *Marks   Code*

1. (*a*) Referring to lines 1–6, give in your own words **two** reasons why the writer finds it surprising that politicians are "telling us not to travel".   2   U

   (*b*) Show how the writer's sentence structure **and** word choice in lines 1–12 convey the strength of her commitment to air travel for all.   4   A

2. Referring to specific words and/or phrases, show how the sentence "So, before . . . as a whole?" (lines 13–14) performs a linking function in the writer's argument.   2   U

3. Read lines 15–23.

   (*a*) What, according to the writer, is the result of "Clamping down on one form of movement"? Use your own words in your answer.   1   U

   (*b*) Explain how the writer uses the example of the London congestion charge to demonstrate her point.   2   U

4. In the paragraph from lines 24 to 28, the writer states that "The only solution . . . is for none of us to go anywhere." (lines 24–25)

   (*a*) Why, according to the writer, is this "solution" undesirable?   2   U

   (*b*) Show how, in this paragraph, the writer creates a tone which conveys her disapproval of the "solution".   2   A

5. Read lines 29–47.

   (*a*) Why, according to the writer, would "never leaving your house" still involve some "ecological guilt"?   1   U

   (*b*) Using your own words as far as possible, summarise the benefits of technology as described in lines 35–43.   3   U

   (*c*) Show how the writer uses sentence structure in lines 35–43 to strengthen her argument.   2   A

   (*d*) What, according to the writer in lines 44–47, would be the outcome of the restrictions proposed by politicians?   2   U

6. Read lines 48–68.

   (*a*) What does the phrase "doomsday scenario" (line 51) mean?   1   U

   (*b*) In your own words, outline the "doomsday scenario" predicted by Thomas Malthus.   2   U

   (*c*) In your own words, give any **two** reasons why Malthus's theory proved incorrect.   2   U

7. How effective do you find the writer's use of language in the final paragraph (lines 69–74) in emphasising her opposition to placing restrictions on people's way of life?   2   A/E

                                                                    (30)

Questions on Passage 2

			Marks	Code

8. (a) Explain the cause of the writer's "depression" (line 4).　　　　　　　2　U

(b) Show how the writer's use of language in lines 1–8 creates an emotional appeal to the reader.　　　　2　A

9. Read lines 9–24.

(a) Explain the "irony" referred to in line 11.　　　　1　U

(b) Show how the writer's use of language in lines 13–19 conveys his unsympathetic view of the speakers at the conference. In your answer you should refer to at least **two** features such as sentence structure, tone, word choice . . .　　　　4　A

(c) How effective do you find the writer's use of imagery in lines 20–24 in conveying the impact that flying has on the environment?　　　　2　A/E

10. Explain why the writer believes that "flying will simply have to become more expensive" (line 30).　　　　2　U

11. Show how the writer, in lines 35–39, creates a dismissive tone when discussing possible remedies.　　　　2　A

(15)

Question on both Passages

12. Which passage is more effective in engaging your interest in aspects of the environmental debate?

Justify your choice by referring to the **ideas and style** of **both passages**.　　　　5　E

(5)

Total (50)

[END OF QUESTION PAPER]

[BLANK PAGE]

X115/303

NATIONAL
QUALIFICATIONS
2009

FRIDAY, 15 MAY
11.05 AM – 12.35 PM

ENGLISH
HIGHER
Critical Essay

Answer **two** questions.

Each question must be taken from a different section.

Each question is worth 25 marks.

Answer TWO questions from this paper. Each question must be chosen from a different Section (A–E). You are not allowed to choose two questions from the same Section.

In all Sections you may use Scottish texts.

Write the number of each question in the margin of your answer booklet and begin each essay on a fresh page.

You should spend about 45 minutes on each essay.

The following will be assessed:

- the relevance of your essays to the questions you have chosen, and the extent to which you sustain an appropriate line of thought

- your knowledge and understanding of key elements, central concerns and significant details of the chosen texts, supported by detailed and relevant evidence

- your understanding, as appropriate to the questions chosen, of how relevant aspects of structure/style/language contribute to the meaning/effect/impact of the chosen texts, supported by detailed and relevant evidence

- your evaluation, as appropriate to the questions chosen, of the effectiveness of the chosen texts, supported by detailed and relevant evidence

- the quality of your written expression and the technical accuracy of your writing.

SECTION A—DRAMA

Answers to questions on drama should address relevantly the central concern(s)/theme(s) of the text and be supported by reference to appropriate dramatic techniques such as: conflict, characterisation, key scene(s), dialogue, climax, exposition, dénouement, structure, plot, setting, aspects of staging (such as lighting, music, stage set, stage directions . . .), soliloquy, monologue . . .

1. Choose a play in which a central character behaves in an obsessive manner.

    Describe the nature of the character's obsessive behaviour and discuss the influence this behaviour has on your understanding of the character in the play as a whole.

2. Choose a play which you feel is made particularly effective by features of structure such as: dramatic opening, exposition, flashback, contrast, turning-point, climax, anticlimax, dénouement . . .

    Show how one or more than one structural feature employed by the dramatist adds to the impact of the play.

3. Choose from a play a scene which significantly changes your view of a character.

    Explain how the scene prompts this reappraisal and discuss how important it is to your understanding of the character in the play as a whole.

4. Choose a play set in a society whose values conflict with those of a central character or characters.

    Describe this difference in values and discuss how effectively the opposition of values enhances your appreciation of the play as a whole.

SECTION B—PROSE

Prose Fiction

> *Answers to questions on prose fiction should address relevantly the central concern(s)/theme(s) of the text(s) and be supported by reference to appropriate techniques of prose fiction such as: characterisation, setting, key incident(s), narrative technique, symbolism, structure, climax, plot, atmosphere, dialogue, imagery . . .*

5. Choose a **novel** or **short story** which deals with true love, unrequited love or love betrayed.

    Discuss the writer's exploration of the theme and show to what extent it conveys a powerful message about the nature of love.

6. Choose a **novel** or **short story** with a central character you consider to be heroic.

    Show how the heroic qualities are revealed and discuss how this portrayal of the character enhances your understanding of the text as a whole.

7. Choose a **novel** in which the setting in time and/or place is a significant feature.

    Show how the writer's use of setting contributes to your understanding of character and theme.

8. Choose a **novel** in which there is an incident involving envy or rivalry or distrust.

    Explain the nature of the incident and go on to discuss its importance to your understanding of the novel as a whole.

Prose Non-fiction

> *Answers to questions on prose non-fiction should address relevantly the central concern(s)/theme(s) of the text and be supported by reference to appropriate techniques of prose non-fiction such as: ideas, use of evidence, selection of detail, point of view, stance, setting, anecdote, narrative voice, style, language, structure, organisation of material . . .*

9. Choose an **essay** or a **piece of journalism** in which you feel that the writer's style is a key factor in developing a persuasive argument.

    Show how the writer's presentation of the argument is made persuasive by his or her use of techniques of non-fiction.

10. Choose a **full-length work** of **biography** or of **autobiography** in which the writer presents the life of her or his subject in a positive light.

    Show how the writer's style and skilful selection of material contribute to this positive portrayal.

11. Choose a **non-fiction text** which exploits the humour of particular situations and/or incidents.

    Show how the writer's use of humour creates interest in the subject matter.

SECTION C—POETRY

Answers to questions on poetry should address relevantly the central concern(s)/theme(s) of the text(s) and be supported by reference to appropriate poetic techniques such as: imagery, verse form, structure, mood, tone, sound, rhythm, rhyme, characterisation, contrast, setting, symbolism, word choice . . .

12. Choose a poem in which the poet explores one of the following emotions: anguish, dissatisfaction, regret, loss.

    Show how the poet explores the emotion and discuss to what extent he or she is successful in deepening your understanding of it.

13. Choose **two** poems which explore the experience of war.

    Discuss which you find more effective in conveying the experience of war.

14. Choose a poem in which contrast is important in developing theme.

    Explore the poet's use of contrast and show why it is important in developing a key theme of the poem.

15. Choose a poem which depicts a particular stage of life, such as childhood, adolescence, middle age, old age.

    Discuss how effectively the poet evokes the essence of this stage of life.

SECTION D—FILM AND TV DRAMA

> *Answers to questions on film and TV drama should address relevantly the central concern(s)/theme(s) of the text(s) and be supported by reference to appropriate techniques of film and TV drama such as: key sequence(s), characterisation, conflict, structure, plot, dialogue, editing/montage, sound/soundtrack, aspects of mise-en-scène (such as lighting, colour, use of camera, costume, props . . .), mood, setting, casting, exploitation of genre . . .*

16. Choose a **film** or **TV drama*** in which two characters are involved in a psychological conflict which dominates the text.

    Show how the film or programme makers reveal the nature of the conflict and explain why it is so significant to the text as a whole.

17. Choose from a **film** an important sequence in which excitement is created as much by filmic technique as by action and dialogue.

    Show how the film makers create this excitement and explain why the sequence is so important to the film as a whole.

18. Choose a **film** or **TV drama*** which evokes a particular period of history and explores significant concerns of life at that time.

    By referring to selected sequences and to the text as a whole, show how the film or programme makers evoke the period and explore significant concerns of life at that time.

19. Choose one or more than one **film** which in your opinion demonstrate(s) outstanding work by a particular director.

    By referring to key elements of the text(s), show why you consider the work of this director to be so impressive.

*"TV drama" includes a single play, a series or a serial.

[Turn over

SECTION E—LANGUAGE

Answers to questions on language should address relevantly the central concern(s) of the language research/study and be supported by reference to appropriate language concepts such as: register, jargon, tone, vocabulary, word choice, technical terminology, presentation, illustration, accent, grammar, idiom, slang, dialect, structure, point of view, orthography, abbreviation . . .

20. Consider aspects of language which change over time, such as slang, idiom, dialect . . .

    Identify some of the changes and discuss to what extent you feel these changes contribute towards possible problems in communication between different age groups or generations.

21. Consider some of the changes in language which have occurred as a result of lobbying by pressure groups such as feminists, multi-cultural organisations, faith groups . . .

    By examining specific examples, discuss to what extent you feel that clarity of communication has been affected by such changes.

22. Consider the use of persuasive language in the promotion of goods or services or a campaign or a cause.

    By examining specific examples, evaluate the success of the language in achieving its purpose.

23. Consider the technical language associated with a sport, a craft, a profession or one of the arts.

    By examining specific examples, discuss to what extent you feel such language leads to clearer communication.

[END OF QUESTION PAPER]

[BLANK PAGE]

X115/301

NATIONAL
QUALIFICATIONS
2010

WEDNESDAY, 12 MAY
9.00 AM – 10.45 AM

ENGLISH
HIGHER
Close Reading—Text

There are TWO passages and questions.

Read the passages carefully and then answer all the questions, which are printed in a separate booklet.

You should read the passages to:

understand what the writers are saying about the changing nature of cities (**Understanding—U**);

analyse their choices of language, imagery and structures to recognise how they convey their points of view and contribute to the impact of the passage (**Analysis—A**);

evaluate how effectively they have achieved their purpose (**Evaluation—E**).

PASSAGE 1

In this passage, the journalist Deyan Sudjic, writing in The Observer *newspaper in March 2008, considers the irresistible growth of cities in the modern world.*

THE FUTURE OF THE CITY

In a world changing faster now than ever before, the dispossessed and the ambitious are flooding into cities swollen out of all recognition. Poor cities are struggling to cope. Rich cities are reconfiguring themselves at breakneck speed. China has created an industrial powerhouse from what were fishing villages in the 1970s. Lagos and Dhaka
5 attract a thousand new arrivals every day. In Britain, central London's population has started to grow again after 50 years of decline.

We have more big cities now than at any time in our history. In 1900, only sixteen had a population of one million; now it's more than 400. Not only are there more of them, they are larger than ever. In 1851, London had two million people. It was the largest
10 city in the world by a long way, twice the size of Paris, its nearest rival. That version of London would seem like a village now. By the official definition, London has getting on for eight million people, but in practical terms, it's a city of 18 million, straggling most of the way from Ipswich to Bournemouth in an unforgiving rash of business parks and designer outlets, gated housing and logistics depots.

15 Having invented the modern city, 19th century Britain promptly reeled back in horror at what it had done. To the Victorians exploring the cholera-ridden back alleys of London's East End, the city was a hideous tumour sucking the life out of the countryside and creating in its place a vast polluted landscape of squalor, disease and crime. In their eyes, the city was a place to be feared, controlled and, if possible,
20 eliminated.

Such attitudes continue to shape thinking about the city. Yet, like it or not, at some point in 2008, the city finally swallowed the world. The number of people living in cities overtook those left behind in the fields. It's a statistic that seems to suggest some sort of fundamental species change, like the moment when mankind stopped being
25 hunter gatherers and took up agriculture.

The future of the city has suddenly become the only subject in town. It ranges from tough topics such as managing water resources, economic policy, transport planning, racial tolerance and law enforcement to what is usually presented as the fluffier end of the scale, such as making public spaces people want to spend time in and deciding the
30 colour of the buses. But it is this diversity which powerfully affirms the city as mankind's greatest single invention.

For all their agonies, cities must be counted as a positive force. They are an engine of growth, a machine for putting the rural poor onto the first rung of urban prosperity and freedom. Look at London, a city that existed for several centuries before anything
35 approximating England had been thought of. It has a far stronger sense of itself and its identity than Britain as a whole or England. It has grown, layer on layer, for 2000 years, sustaining generation after generation of newcomers.

You see their traces in the Spitalfields district, where a French Huguenot chapel became, successively, a synagogue and a mosque, tracking the movement of waves of
40 migrants from poverty to suburban comfort. London's a place without an apparent structure that has proved extraordinarily successful at growing and changing. Its old residential core, sheltering in the approaches to its Tower of London fortress, has made the transition into the world's busiest banking centre. Its market halls and power stations have become art galleries and piazzas. Its simple terraced streets, built for the

45 clerks of the Great Western Railway in Southall, have become home to the largest Sikh community outside India.

And all of these worlds overlap in space and time. London is different for all its people. They make the most of the elements in it that have meaning for them and ignore the rest. A city is an à la carte menu. That is what makes it different from a village, which 50 has little room for tolerance and difference. And a great city is one in which as many people as possible can make the widest of choices from its menu.

The cities that work best are those that keep their options open, that allow the possibility of change. The ones that are stuck, overwhelmed by rigid, state-owned social housing, or by economic systems that offer the poor no way out of the slums, are 55 in trouble. A successful city is one that makes room for surprises. A city that has been trapped by too much gentrification or too many shopping malls will have trouble generating the spark that is essential to making a city that works.

Successful cities are the ones that allow people to be what they want; unsuccessful ones try to force them to be what others want them to be. A city of freeways like Houston or 60 Los Angeles forces people to be car drivers or else traps them in poverty. A successful city has a public transport system that is easy to use; an unsuccessful city tries to ban cars.

A successful city has room for more than the obvious ideas about city life, because, in the end, a city is about the unexpected, about a life shared with strangers and open to 65 new ideas. An unsuccessful city has closed its mind to the future.

PASSAGE 2

The following passage is adapted from The Dreaming City, *a report about Glasgow's future produced by a political "think tank" in 2007.*

Glasgow is a city which has experienced constant change and adaptation, from its period as a great industrial city and as the Second City of Empire, to its latter day reinvention as the City of Culture and the Second City of Shopping. This is a city with pull, buzz, excitement, and a sense of style and its own importance. It has a 5 potent international reach and influence. Glasgow's story continually weaves in and out of a global urban tapestry: following the trade threads of Empire, there are nearly two dozen towns and cities around the world named after Glasgow—from Jamaica to Montana to Nova Scotia. And there is even a Glasgow on the moon.

Glasgow's constant proclamation of its present success story is justified on the basis 10 that it benefits the city: confidence will breed confidence, tourists will visit, businesses will relocate and students will enrol. But, despite the gains this approach has brought for Glasgow and cities like it, there are signs that the wind is starting to come out of the sails. What felt radical when Dublin, Barcelona and Glasgow embarked on the city makeover path in the late 1980s and early 1990s, now feels derivative and is delivering 15 diminishing returns. When every city has commissioned a celebrity architect and pedestrianised a cultural quarter, distinctiveness is reduced to a formula.

Yet "official" Glasgow continues to celebrate its new-found status as a shopping mecca and top tourist destination, revelling in the city's new role as a place for conspicuous consumption, affluent lifestyles and global city breaks. There are several problems 20 with this. One is that this is a city with historic and deep inequalities, a city of sharp

divisions in income, employment, life chances and health. Another is that it can be seen as promoting a way of living that is unsustainable in terms of people's disposable income and growing levels of debt. And yet another problem is the clutter of cities on the world-class trail with the same familiar formula supporting
25 their campaign—shopping, tourism, mega-events, cultural events, iconic architecture and casinos—leaving little room for distinctiveness.

The politicians and the Establishment talk the language of "opportunity", "choice" and "diversity" for the people of the city, but do not really believe in or practise them. They impose a set menu, rather than the choice offered "à la carte",
30 confident that they know best. For all the rhetoric about new ways of working, partnership and collaboration, there can still be a very old-fashioned top-down approach in parts of institutional Glasgow that retains a faith that experts and professionals must hold all the answers. There is an implicit belief that people are poor because of low aspirations and Glaswegians are unhealthy because they won't
35 accept responsibility, make the right choices and eat healthily.

This dichotomy between the powerful and the powerless undermines the whole concept of the "resurgence" of cities such as Glasgow. At the moment, the city and its people only come together for mega-events such as the Commonwealth Games or City of Music bids. The question is whether this unity can be mobilised in a more
40 sustained way. There is an urgent need to find some new shared values and vision to help bridge the gap between the city and its people—to close the gap between the cities people want and the cities people get.

[END OF TEXT]

X115/302

NATIONAL
QUALIFICATIONS
2010

WEDNESDAY, 12 MAY
9.00 AM – 10.45 AM

ENGLISH
HIGHER
Close Reading–Questions

Answer all questions.

50 marks are allocated to this paper.

A code letter (U, A, E) is used alongside each question to give some indication of the skills being assessed. The number of marks attached to each question will give some indication of the length of answer required.

When answering questions coded "U—Understanding", use your own words as far as is reasonably possible and do not simply repeat the wording of the passage.

Marks Code

Questions on Passage 1

> *You are reminded of the instruction on the front cover:*
> *When answering questions coded "U—Understanding", use your own words as far as is*
> *reasonably possible and do not simply repeat the wording of the passage.*

1. Read lines 1–6.

    (a) Explain which groups of people are being attracted to cities.   2   U

    (b) Show how any **two** examples of word choice in this paragraph emphasise
    the impact of the growth of cities.   2   A

2. Referring to lines 7–14, explain **two** ways in which "That version of London
    would seem like a village now" (lines 10–11).   2   U

3. Show how the writer's use of language in lines 15–20 conveys the Victorians'
    disgust at the city they had created. You should refer in your answer to such
    features as imagery, word choice, sentence structure . . .   4   A

4. In lines 21–25, the writer tells us that for the first time in history more people
    are now living in cities than in the countryside. Show how the writer's use of
    language in this paragraph emphasises the momentous nature of this change.   2   A

5. Read lines 26–31.

    Explain in detail why the writer thinks the city is "mankind's greatest single
    invention" (line 31).   2   U

6. Read lines 32–37.

    Give any **two** reasons why cities "must be counted as a positive force".   2   U

7. Read lines 38–46.

    (a) Explain how any **one** of the examples in these lines illustrates the
    surprising nature of the way London has changed over time.   2   U

    (b) Show how the sentence structure of the paragraph as a whole emphasises
    the idea of change.   2   A

8. Show how the image of the "à la carte menu" illustrates the point the writer is
    making in lines 47–51.   2   A

9. Read lines 52–65.

    (a) According to the writer, what is the key difference between successful
    cities and unsuccessful cities?   1   U

    (b) Show how the writer's use of language in these lines emphasises this
    difference.   2   A

    (25)

Marks   Code

Questions on Passage 2

> *You are reminded of the instruction on the front cover:*
> *When answering questions coded "U—Understanding", use your own words as far as is*
> *reasonably possible and do not simply repeat the wording of the passage.*

10. Read lines 1–8.

   (*a*) Explain why, according to the writer, Glasgow was in the past an important world city.   **1   U**

   (*b*) Explain why Glasgow could be considered important now.   **1   U**

   (*c*) Show how the writer's use of language in lines 3–8 ("This is a city . . . the moon.") emphasises Glasgow's importance.   **2   A**

11. Read lines 9–16.

   (*a*) What does the writer mean by the words "radical" (line 13) and "derivative" (line 14) in his discussion of city development?   **2   U**

   (*b*) Show how the writer's use of language in lines 9–16 suggests his doubts about the alleged "success story" of Glasgow.   **4   A**

12. Read lines 17–26.

   (*a*) "There are several problems with this." (lines 19–20). Explain briefly what these "problems" are.   **3   U**

   (*b*) Explain fully how the structure of lines 19–26 ("There are . . . room for distinctiveness.") helps to clarify the writer's argument.   **2   A**

13. Read lines 27–35.

   (*a*) What is the writer's main criticism of the way the "politicians and the Establishment" run Glasgow?   **1   U**

   (*b*) Show how the writer's use of language in this paragraph creates a tone of disapproval.   **2   A**

14. Read lines 36–42.

Explain the approach the writer would prefer to see in the way Glasgow is run.   **2   U**

   (20)

Question on both Passages

15. Which passage do you think offers the more thought-provoking ideas about the nature of cities?

Justify your choice by close reference to the **ideas** of **both passages**.   **5   U/E**

   (5)

   Total (50)

[END OF QUESTION PAPER]

[BLANK PAGE]

X115/303

NATIONAL
QUALIFICATIONS
2010

WEDNESDAY, 12 MAY
11.05 AM – 12.35 PM

ENGLISH
HIGHER
Critical Essay

Answer **two** questions.

Each question must be taken from a different section.

Each question is worth 25 marks.

Answer **TWO** questions from this paper. Each question must be chosen from a different Section (A–E). You are not allowed to choose two questions from the same Section.

In all Sections you may use Scottish texts.

Write the number of each question in the margin of your answer booklet and begin each essay on a fresh page.

You should spend about 45 minutes on each essay.

The following will be assessed:

- the relevance of your essays to the questions you have chosen, and the extent to which you sustain an appropriate line of thought

- your knowledge and understanding of key elements, central concerns and significant details of the chosen texts, supported by detailed and relevant evidence

- your understanding, as appropriate to the questions chosen, of how relevant aspects of structure/style/language contribute to the meaning/effect/impact of the chosen texts, supported by detailed and relevant evidence

- your evaluation, as appropriate to the questions chosen, of the effectiveness of the chosen texts, supported by detailed and relevant evidence

- the quality of your written expression and the technical accuracy of your writing.

SECTION A—DRAMA

Answers to questions on drama should address relevantly the central concern(s)/theme(s) of the text and be supported by reference to appropriate dramatic techniques such as: conflict, characterisation, key scene(s), dialogue, climax, exposition, dénouement, structure, plot, setting, aspects of staging (such as lighting, music, stage set, stage directions . . .), soliloquy, monologue . . .

1. Choose a play in which a central concern is clarified by the contrast between two characters.

   Discuss how the dramatist's presentation of the contrast between the two characters adds to your understanding of this central concern.

2. Choose a play in which a central character experiences not only inner conflict but also conflict with one (or more than one) other character.

   Explain the nature of both conflicts and discuss which one you consider to be more important in terms of character development and/or dramatic impact.

3. Choose from a play a scene in which tension builds to a climax.

   Explain how the dramatist creates and develops this tension, and discuss the extent to which the scene has thematic as well as dramatic significance.

4. Choose a play which explores one of the following as a central concern: sacrifice, courage, integrity, steadfastness of purpose.

   Show how the dramatist introduces and develops the central concern in a way which you find effective.

SECTION B—PROSE

Prose Fiction

> *Answers to questions on prose fiction should address relevantly the central concern(s)/theme(s) of the text(s) and be supported by reference to appropriate techniques of prose fiction such as: characterisation, setting, key incident(s), narrative technique, symbolism, structure, climax, plot, atmosphere, dialogue, imagery . . .*

5. Choose a **novel** or **short story** which features a relationship between two characters which is confrontational or corrosive.

    Describe how the relationship is portrayed and discuss to what extent the nature of the relationship influences your understanding of the text as a whole.

6. Choose a **novel** in which the novelist makes use of more than one location.

    Discuss how the use of different locations allows the novelist to develop the central concern(s) of the text.

7. Choose a **novel** in which a character experiences a moment of revelation.

    Describe briefly what is revealed and discuss its significance to your understanding of character and/or theme.

8. Choose a **novel** in which a character seeks to escape from the constraints of his or her environment or situation.

    Explain why the character feels the need to escape and show how his or her response to the situation illuminates a central concern of the text.

9. Choose **two short stories** whose openings are crafted to seize the reader's attention.

    Explain in detail how the impact of the openings is created and go on to evaluate which of the stories develops more successfully from its opening.

Prose Non-fiction

> *Answers to questions on prose non-fiction should address relevantly the central concern(s)/theme(s) of the text and be supported by reference to appropriate techniques of prose non-fiction such as: ideas, use of evidence, selection of detail, point of view, stance, setting, anecdote, narrative voice, style, language, structure, organisation of material . . .*

10. Choose a work of **biography** or of **autobiography** which describes triumph over adversity or triumph over misfortune.

    Show how the writer's presentation of events and details in the subject's life leads you to an appreciation of her or his eventual success.

11. Choose a **non-fiction text** in which the writer's use of structure makes a significant impact.

    Describe the important structural features of the text and show how these enhance the impact of the writer's message.

12. Choose a **non-fiction text** in which vivid description is an important feature.

    Discuss in detail how the vivid description is created and go on to explain how it contributes to your appreciation of the text as a whole.

SECTION C—POETRY

> *Answers to questions on poetry should address relevantly the central concern(s)/theme(s) of the text(s) and be supported by reference to appropriate poetic techniques such as: imagery, verse form, structure, mood, tone, sound, rhythm, rhyme, characterisation, contrast, setting, symbolism, word choice . . .*

13. Choose a poem in which the central concern(s) is/are clarified for you in the closing lines.

Show how these closing lines provide an effective clarification of the central concern(s) of the poem.

14. Choose a poem in which there is an element of ambiguity.

Show how the poet's use of ambiguity enriches your appreciation of the poem as a whole.

15. Choose a poem in which the creation of mood or atmosphere is an important feature.

Show how the poet creates the mood or atmosphere, and discuss its importance in your appreciation of the poem as a whole.

16. Choose **two** poems in which differing stances are adopted on the same subject.

Show how the stances are revealed and discuss which treatment you find more effective.

SECTION D—FILM AND TV DRAMA

> *Answers to questions on film and TV drama should address relevantly the central concern(s)/theme(s) of the text(s) and be supported by reference to appropriate techniques of film and TV drama such as: key sequence(s), characterisation, conflict, structure, plot, dialogue, editing/montage, sound/soundtrack, aspects of mise-en-scène (such as lighting, colour, use of camera, costume, props . . .), mood, setting, casting, exploitation of genre . . .*

17. Choose a **film** or **TV drama*** in which a character overcomes apparently insuperable difficulties.

    Briefly describe these difficulties and go on to discuss how the film or programme makers present the character's success in a way which you find satisfying.

18. Choose a **film** or **TV drama*** in which the opening sequence successfully establishes key features of the text such as setting, mood, genre, character . . .

    By referring to more than one key feature in the sequence, show how the film or programme makers achieve this success and go on to discuss the importance of the sequence to your appreciation of the text as a whole.

19. Choose a **film** or **TV drama*** which portrays a family or group of people with a distinctive set of values.

    Show how the film or programme makers reveal these values and discuss to what extent these contribute to your understanding of theme.

20. Choose a **film** or **TV drama*** which deals with violence but does not glorify it.

    Discuss the film or programme makers' exploration of violence, making clear why you consider the treatment to be acceptable.

*"TV drama" includes a single play, a series or a serial.

[Turn over

SECTION E—LANGUAGE

Answers to questions on language should address relevantly the central concern(s) of the language research/study and be supported by reference to appropriate language concepts such as: register, jargon, tone, vocabulary, word choice, technical terminology, presentation, illustration, accent, grammar, idiom, slang, dialect, structure, point of view, orthography, abbreviation . . .

21. Consider aspects of language shared by members of a vocational group.

Identify some examples of the language used within the group and evaluate the extent to which this shared language contributes to the effectiveness of the group's vocational activities.

22. Consider the language used to promote products, ideas or beliefs.

Identify some of the characteristics of this language and assess how effective it is in promoting these products, ideas or beliefs.

23. Consider the language of broadsheet and/or tabloid newspaper reporting of a specific subject area such as politics, environmental issues, crime, sport, education . . .

Identify some of the characteristics of this language and discuss its effectiveness in reporting on the chosen subject.

24. Consider the spoken language of a specific geographical area.

Identify some of the characteristics of the language of your chosen area and discuss to what extent it enriches community life.

[END OF QUESTION PAPER]

[BLANK PAGE]

X270/301

NATIONAL	FRIDAY, 13 MAY	**ENGLISH**
QUALIFICATIONS	9.00 AM – 10.45 AM	**HIGHER**
2011		Close Reading—Text

There are TWO passages and questions.

Read the passages carefully and then answer all the questions, which are printed in a separate booklet.

You should read the passages to:

understand what the writers are saying about the appeal and influence of video games (**Understanding—U**);

analyse their choices of language, imagery and structures to recognise how they convey their points of view and contribute to the impact of the passage (**Analysis—A**);

evaluate how effectively they have achieved their purpose (**Evaluation—E**).

PASSAGE 1

Writing in The Times *newspaper, Steven Johnson argues that valuable development in young people's mental abilities can come from "popular culture" in general—and video games in particular.*

MAKING OUR BRAINS SHARPER

Reading books enriches the mind; playing video games deadens it—you can't get much more conventional than the conventional wisdom that kids today would be better off spending more time reading books, and less time zoning out in front of their video games.

5 For the record, I think that the virtues of reading books are great. We should all encourage our kids to read more. But even the most avid reader is inevitably going to spend his or her time with other media—games, television, movies, the Internet. Yet the question is whether these other forms of culture have intellectual virtues in their own right—different from, but comparable to, reading. Where most critics allege a
10 dumbing down, I see a progressive story: popular culture steadily, but almost imperceptibly, making our brains sharper as we soak in entertainment usually dismissed as so much lowbrow fluff. I hope to persuade you that increasingly the non-literary popular culture is honing different mental skills that are just as important as the ones exercised by reading books.

15 The most powerful example of this trend is found in the world of video games. And the first and last thing that should be said about the experience of playing today's video games, the thing you almost never hear, is that games are fiendishly, sometimes maddeningly, hard. The dirty little secret of gaming is how much time you spend not having fun. You may be frustrated; you may be confused or disorientated; you may be
20 stuck. But when you put the game down and move back into the real world, you may find yourself mentally working through the problem you have been wrestling with, as though you were worrying a loose tooth.

In the typical game, the tasks themselves are more like chores than entertainment. And yet ironically the great bulk of the population performing these tasks every day is
25 composed of precisely the demographic group most averse to doing chores: kids whom you virtually have to lock in their room to get them to do their maths homework. You often hear video games included in the list of the debased instant gratifications that abound in our culture. But compared with most forms of popular entertainment, games turn out to be all about delayed gratification, sometimes so long delayed that you
30 wonder if the gratification is ever going to show.

So why does anyone bother playing these things? And why does a seven-year-old soak up, for instance, the intricacies of industrial economics in the game form of SimCity, when the same subject would send him screaming for the exits in a classroom? To date, there has been little direct research into the question of how games get children to learn
35 without realising that they are learning. But I believe a strong case can be made that the power of games to captivate largely involves their ability to tap into the brain's natural reward circuitry. If you create a system in which rewards are both clearly defined and achieved by exploring an environment, you will find human brains drawn to those systems, even if they are made up of virtual characters and simulated sidewalks.
40 In the game world, reward is everywhere. The gaming universe is literally teeming with objects that deliver very clearly articulated rewards: more life, access to new levels, new equipment, new spells. Most of the crucial work in game design focuses on keeping players notified of potential rewards available to them, and how much these

rewards are currently needed. Most games offer a fictional world where rewards are
45 larger, and more vivid, and more clearly defined than life.

You may just want to win the game, of course, or perhaps you want to see the game's
narrative completed, or in the initial stages of play, you may just be dazzled by the
game's graphics. But most of the time, when you're hooked on a game, what draws you
in is an elemental form of desire: the desire to see the Next Thing. After all, with the
50 occasional exception, the actual content of the game is often childish or gratuitously
menacing. Much of the role play inside the gaming world alternates between drive-by
shooting and princess-rescuing. It is not the subject matter that attracts; it is the
reward system that draws those players in, and keeps their famously short attention
spans locked on the screen.

55 Playing down the content of video games shouldn't be seen as a cop-out. We ignore the
content of many other activities that are widely considered to be good for the brain. No
one complains about the simplistic, militaristic plot of chess games. We teach algebra
to children knowing full well that the day they leave the classroom 99 per cent of those
kids will never again directly employ their algebraic skills. Learning algebra isn't about
60 acquiring a specific tool; it's about building up a mental muscle that will come in handy
elsewhere.

So it is with games. It's not what you're thinking about when you're playing a game,
it's the way you're thinking that matters. Novels may activate our imagination and may
conjure up powerful emotions, but games force you to analyse, to choose, to prioritise,
65 to decide. From the outside, the primary activity of a gamer looks like a fury of clicking
and shooting. But if you peer inside the gamer's mind, the primary activity turns out to
be another creature altogether: making decisions, some of them snap judgements, some
of them long-term strategies.

PASSAGE 2

Writing in The Daily Telegraph *(2006), the politician and journalist Boris Johnson blames
video games for a drop in reading standards.*

STRIKE A BLOW FOR LITERACY

It's the snarl that gives the game away. It's the sobbing and the shrieking and the
horrible pleading—that's how you know your children are undergoing a sudden
narcotic withdrawal. As the strobing colours die away and the screen goes black, you
listen to the wail of protest from the offspring and you know that you have just turned
5 off their drug, and you know that they are, to a greater or lesser extent, addicts.

Millions of seven-to-fifteen-year olds are hooked, especially boys, and it is time
someone had the guts to stand up, cross the room and just say no to Nintendo. It is
time to garrotte the Game Boy and paralyse the PlayStation, and it is about time, as a
society, that we admitted the catastrophic effect these blasted gizmos are having on the
10 literacy and the prospects of young males.

We demand that teachers provide our children with reading skills; we expect the
schools to fill them with a love of books; and yet at home we let them slump in front of
the consoles. We get on with our hedonistic 21st century lives while in some other
room the nippers are bleeping and zapping in speechless rapture, their passive faces

15 washed in explosions and gore. They sit for so long that their souls seem to have
been sucked down the cathode ray tube.

They become like blinking lizards, motionless, absorbed, only the twitching of their
hands showing that they are still conscious. These machines teach them nothing.
They stimulate no ratiocination, discovery or feat of memory—though some of them
20 may cunningly pretend to be educational. I have just watched an eleven-year-old
play a game that looked fairly historical, on the packet. Your average guilt-ridden
parent might assume that it taught the child something about the Vikings and
medieval siege warfare. Phooey! The red soldiers robotically slaughtered the white
soldiers, and then they did it again, that was it. Everything was programmed,
25 spoon-fed, immediate—and endlessly showering the player with undeserved praise,
richly congratulating him for his bogus massacres.

The more addictive these games are to the male mind, the more difficult it is to
persuade boys to read books. It's not that these young people lack the brains; the
raw circuitry is better than ever. It's the software that's the problem. They have not
30 been properly programmed, because they have not read enough. The only way to
learn to write is to be forced time and again to articulate your own thoughts in your
own words, and you haven't a hope of doing this if you haven't read enough to
absorb the basic elements of vocabulary, grammar, rhythm, style and structure; and
young males in particular won't read enough if we continually capitulate and let
35 them fritter their lives away in front of these drivelling machines.

So I say now: go to where your children are sitting in auto-lobotomy in front of the
console. Summon up all your strength, all your courage. Steel yourself for the
screams and yank out that plug. And if they still kick up a fuss, then get out the
sledgehammer and strike a blow for literacy.

[END OF TEXT]

X270/302

NATIONAL
QUALIFICATIONS
2011

FRIDAY, 13 MAY
9.00 AM – 10.45 AM

ENGLISH
HIGHER
Close Reading–Questions

Answer all questions.

50 marks are allocated to this paper.

A code letter (U, A, E) is used alongside each question to give some indication of the skills being assessed. The number of marks attached to each question will give some indication of the length of answer required.

When answering questions coded "U—Understanding", use your own words as far as is reasonably possible and do not simply repeat the wording of the passage.

Marks Code

Questions on Passage 1

> *You are reminded of the instruction on the front cover:*
> *When answering questions coded "U—Understanding", use your own words as far as is*
> *reasonably possible and do not simply repeat the wording of the passage.*

1. Read lines 1–14.

    (a) Show how the writer's word choice in lines 1–4 emphasises the "conventional wisdom" that reading books is better than playing video games.   2   A

    (b) Explain "the question" the writer asks in lines 7–9 about "other forms of culture".   2   U

    (c) Show how the writer's use of language in lines 9–14 ("Where . . . books.") emphasises the contrast between his positive view of "other forms of culture" and the negative view held by "most critics".

    In your answer you should refer to specific language features such as imagery, word choice, sentence structure . . .   4   A

2. ". . . how much time you spend not having fun." (lines 18–19)

    Show how, in lines 15–22, the writer conveys the difficulty of playing video games by his use of:

    (a) sentence structure;   2   A

    (b) imagery.   2   A

3. Read lines 23–30.

    (a) What is ironic about the situation described by the writer in lines 23–26 ("In the typical game . . . homework.")?   1   U

    (b) In lines 26–30 ("You often . . . show."), what distinction does the writer make between video games and "most forms of popular entertainment"?   2   U

4. Read lines 31–45.

    (a) According to the writer, why is "reward" so important to the learning process involved in playing video games?   3   U

    (b) Show how the writer's use of language in lines 40–45 ("In the game world . . . life.") conveys the excitement generated by rewards in the world of video games.   2   A

5. Read lines 46–54.

    (a) Give two criticisms the writer makes of the content of video games.   2   U

    (b) Show how the writer's use of language in these lines conveys a dismissive attitude towards the content of video games.   2   A

6. How does the example of algebra **or** of chess illustrate the point the writer is making in lines 55–61?   2   U

Marks   Code

7. Read lines 62–68.

   (*a*) "Novels may activate our imagination and may conjure up powerful emotions, but games force you to analyse, to choose, to prioritise, to decide." (lines 63–65)

   Show how the writer's use of language in this sentence emphasises the contrast between novels and video games.

   2   A

   (*b*) Show how the writer's use of language in lines 65–68 conveys the contrast between what a gamer looks like from "the outside" and what is happening "inside the gamer's mind".

   2   A

   (30)

Questions on Passage 2

You are reminded of the instruction on the front cover:
When answering questions coded "U—Understanding", use your own words as far as is reasonably possible and do not simply repeat the wording of the passage.

8. Read lines 1–10.

   (*a*) In what ways, according to the writer, can young people be adversely affected by playing video games?

   2   U

   (*b*) Show how the writer creates in these lines an impression of outrage in his condemnation of video games.

   2   A

9. Show how the writer's word choice in lines 11–16 reinforces the contrast he is creating between school and home.

   2   A

10. Show how the writer's use of language in lines 17–26 conveys his contempt for the claim that there is some educational value in some video games.

   4   A

11. Read lines 27–35.

   Why, according to the writer, is reading important in the development of writing skills?

   2   U

12. How effective do you find lines 36–39 as a conclusion to the writer's condemnation of video gaming in the passage as a whole?

   3   E

   (15)

Question on both Passages

13. Which passage gives you a more interesting insight into the appeal and influence of video games?

   Justify your choice by referring to the **ideas** of **both passages**.

   5   U/E

   (5)

   Total (50)

[END OF QUESTION PAPER]

[BLANK PAGE]

X270/303

NATIONAL
QUALIFICATIONS
2011

FRIDAY, 13 MAY
11.05 AM – 12.35 PM

ENGLISH
HIGHER
Critical Essay

Answer **two** questions.

Each question must be taken from a different section.

Each question is worth 25 marks.

Answer TWO questions from this paper. Each question must be chosen from a different Section (A–E). You are not allowed to choose two questions from the same Section.

In all Sections you may use Scottish texts.

Write the number of each question in the margin of your answer booklet and begin each essay on a fresh page.

You should spend about 45 minutes on each essay.

The following will be assessed:

- the relevance of your essays to the questions you have chosen, and the extent to which you sustain an appropriate line of thought

   your knowledge and understanding of key elements, central concerns and significant details of the chosen texts, supported by detailed and relevant evidence

   your understanding, as appropriate to the questions chosen, of how relevant aspects of structure/style/language contribute to the meaning/effect/impact of the chosen texts, supported by detailed and relevant evidence

   your evaluation, as appropriate to the questions chosen, of the effectiveness of the chosen texts, supported by detailed and relevant evidence

   the quality of your written expression and the technical accuracy of your writing.

SECTION A—DRAMA

Answers to questions on drama should address relevantly the central concern(s)/theme(s) of the text and be supported by reference to appropriate dramatic techniques such as: conflict, characterisation, key scene(s), dialogue, climax, exposition, dénouement, structure, plot, setting, aspects of staging (such as lighting, music, stage set, stage directions . . .), soliloquy, monologue . . .

1. Choose a play in which a character feels insecure about his or her position within the society or social group to which he or she belongs.

   Show how the dramatist makes you aware of the character's insecurity and discuss how it influences your appreciation of character and/or theme in the play as a whole.

2. Choose from a play a scene in which manipulation, temptation or humiliation is an important feature.

   Explain what happens in the scene and go on to show how the outcome of the manipulation, temptation or humiliation adds to your appreciation of the play as a whole.

3. Choose a play in which the dramatist creates tension at the beginning or at the end.

   Explain how the tension is created and discuss how it contributes to an effective introduction or conclusion to the play.

4. Choose a play in which a power struggle is central to the action.

   Explain briefly the circumstances of the power struggle and discuss the extent to which it contributes to your appreciation of theme and/or character in the play as a whole.

SECTION B—PROSE

Prose Fiction

Answers to questions on prose fiction should address relevantly the central concern(s)/theme(s) of the text(s) and be supported by reference to appropriate techniques of prose fiction such as: characterisation, setting, key incident(s), narrative technique, symbolism, structure, climax, plot, atmosphere, dialogue, imagery . . .

5. Choose a **novel** in which friendship or love is put to the test.

   Explain briefly how this situation arises and go on to discuss how the outcome of the test leads you to a greater understanding of the central concern(s) of the text.

6. Choose a **novel** in which a central character is flawed but remains an admirable figure.

   Show how the writer makes you aware of these aspects of personality and discuss how this feature of characterisation enhances your appreciation of the text as a whole.

7. Choose a **novel** or **short story** in which the writer explores feelings of rejection or isolation or alienation.

   Explain how the writer makes you aware of these feelings and go on to show how this exploration enhances your appreciation of the text as a whole.

8. Choose a **novel** in which the narrative point of view is a significant feature in your appreciation of the text.

   Show how the writer's use of this feature enhances your understanding of the central concern(s) of the text.

9. Choose **two short stories** in which setting plays an important role in developing your understanding of character and/or theme.

   Which story, in your opinion, is more effective in developing your understanding? Justify your choice by reference to the setting of both stories.

[Turn over for Prose Non-fiction

SECTION B—PROSE (continued)

Prose Non-fiction

> *Answers to questions on prose non-fiction should address relevantly the central concern(s)/theme(s) of the text and be supported by reference to appropriate techniques of prose non-fiction such as: ideas, use of evidence, selection of detail, point of view, stance, setting, anecdote, narrative voice, style, language, structure, organisation of material . . .*

10. Choose a **non-fiction text** in which the writer expresses outrage or shock about an issue which you feel is important.

    Show how the writer conveys the emotion and discuss to what extent this emotional approach enhances your understanding of the issue.

11. Choose a **biography** or **autobiography** in which the writer brings more than one key incident vividly to life.

    Show how the writer brings the incidents vividly to life and explain how they contribute to your overall understanding of the person involved.

12. Choose a **non-fiction text** whose tone is either very optimistic or very pessimistic.

    Show how the tone is created and discuss to what extent it is effective in developing the theme of the text.

SECTION C—POETRY

Answers to questions on poetry should address relevantly the central concern(s)/theme(s) of the text(s) and be supported by reference to appropriate poetic techniques such as: imagery, verse form, structure, mood, tone, sound, rhythm, rhyme, characterisation, contrast, setting, symbolism, word choice . . .

13. Choose a poem which seems to you to be critical of a person or a point of view.

    Discuss how effectively this criticism is presented by the poet.

14. Choose a poem in which the poet blends narration and reflection.

    Show how the poet blends these two aspects in such a way as to illuminate the central concern(s) of the poem.

15. Choose a poem in which **either** nature **or** time is presented as a destructive force.

    Discuss how effectively the poet presents nature **or** time in this way.

16. Choose a poem in which the tone is sinister **or** seductive **or** cynical.

    Show how the poem creates this tone and discuss its relative importance in your appreciation of the poem.

[Turn over

SECTION D—FILM AND TV DRAMA

> *Answers to questions on film and TV drama should address relevantly the central concern(s)/theme(s) of the text(s) and be supported by reference to appropriate techniques of film and TV drama such as: key sequence(s), characterisation, conflict, structure, plot, dialogue, editing/montage, sound/soundtrack, aspects of mise-en-scène (such as lighting, colour, use of camera, costume, props . . .), mood, setting, casting, exploitation of genre . . .*

17. Choose a **film** or **TV drama*** in which a character overcomes or gives way to temptation.

Discuss how the film or programme makers use this situation to influence your emotional and intellectual response to the text as a whole.

18. Choose a **film** or **TV drama*** containing a sequence you find disturbing or unsettling.

Show how the film or programme makers achieve this response and go on to discuss the importance of the sequence to your appreciation of the text as a whole.

19. Choose a **film** or **TV drama*** in which setting has a significant influence on mood and theme.

Show how the film or programme makers reveal this setting and discuss why it is so influential in terms of mood and theme.

20. Choose a **film** or **TV drama*** which celebrates the triumph of the human spirit.

Show how the film or programme makers explore this theme and discuss how a sense of celebration is achieved.

*"TV drama" includes a single play, a series or a serial.

SECTION E—LANGUAGE

Answers to questions on language should address relevantly the central concern(s) of the language research/study and be supported by reference to appropriate language concepts such as: register, jargon, tone, vocabulary, word choice, technical terminology, presentation, illustration, accent, grammar, idiom, slang, dialect, structure, point of view, orthography, abbreviation . . .

21. Consider aspects of language within a specific interest group.

Identify aspects of language which are typical of this group and discuss to what extent these aspects of language operate to the advantage of its members.

22. Consider some of the ways in which language differs across generations.

Identify some of these differences and the factors which cause them. Go on to discuss to what extent this is advantageous to those involved.

23. Consider the language of television programmes **or** radio programmes **or** magazines **or** websites which are aimed at an audience defined by such features as shared cultural or leisure or political interests.

Identify some of the characteristics of the language and evaluate its effectiveness in communicating with its target audience.

24. Consider the spoken and/or written language used by people who exercise power effectively.

Identify what is distinctive about the language and discuss why it is effective in influencing its audience.

[END OF QUESTION PAPER]

[BLANK PAGE]

PUBLISHER'S NOTE

Unfortunately, due to copyright reasons, we are unable to publish the text of the 2012 Close Reading papers. We have substituted this with the text of the most recent Specimen Question Papers – see the following pages 71–78. We apologise for any inconvenience this may cause.

[C270/SQP273]

English	Time: 1 hour 45 minutes	NATIONAL
Higher		QUALIFICATIONS

Close Reading—Text
Specimen Question Paper

There are TWO passages and questions.

Read both passages carefully and then answer all the questions, which are printed in a separate booklet.

You should read the passages to:

understand what the authors are saying about the proposal to put online the contents of some major libraries **(Understanding—U)**;

analyse their choices of language, imagery and structures to recognise how they convey their

points of view and contribute to the impact of the passages **(Analysis—A)**;

evaluate how effectively they have achieved their purposes **(Evaluation—E)**.

SQA

PASSAGE 1

In the first passage George Kerevan, writing in The Scotsman newspaper in December 2004, responds to the prospect of an "online library" and explains the importance to him of the type of library we have at the moment.

DESPITE GOOGLE, WE STILL NEED GOOD LIBRARIES

The internet search engine Google, with whom I spend more time than with my loved ones, is planning to put the contents of the world's greatest university libraries online, including the Bodleian in Oxford and those of Harvard and Stanford in America. Part of me is ecstatic at the thought of all that information at my fingertips; another part of
5 me is nostalgic, because I think physical libraries, book-lined and cathedral-quiet, are a cherished part of civilisation we lose at our cultural peril.

My love affair with libraries started early, in the Drumchapel housing scheme in the Fifties. For the 60,000 exiles packed off from slum housing to the city's outer fringe, Glasgow Council neglected the shops and amenities but somehow remembered to put
10 in a public library—actually, a wooden shed. That library was split into two—an adult section and a children's section. This was an early taste of forbidden fruit. Much useful human reproductive knowledge was gained from certain books examined surreptitiously in the adult biology section.

At university, I discovered the wonder of the library as a physical space. Glasgow
15 University has a skyscraper library, built around a vast atrium stretching up through the various floors. Each floor was devoted to a different subject classification. Working away on the economics floor, I could see other students above or below—chatting, flirting, doodling, panicking—all cocooned in their own separate worlds of knowledge. Intrigued, I soon took to exploring what was on these other planets: science, architecture,
20 even a whole floor of novels. The unique aspect of a physical library is that you can discover knowledge by accident. There are things you know you don't know, but there are also things you never imagined you did not know.

There is a stock response to my love affair with libraries: that I am being too nostalgic. That the multi-tasking, MTV generation can access information from a computer, get
25 cheap books from the supermarket and still chatter to each other at a thousand decibels. Who needs old-fashioned library buildings? And why should councils subsidise what Google will provide for free?

There is some proof for this line of argument. The number of people in Scotland using their local public library falls every year, with just under a quarter of Scots now
30 borrowing books (admittedly, that was 34 million books). As a result, local authorities have reduced their funding for new books by 30 per cent. Of course, fewer new books mean fewer library users, so guaranteeing the downward spiral.

It may well be that public demand and technical change mean we no longer need the dense neighbourhood network of local libraries of yore. But our culture, local and
35 universal, does demand strategically situated libraries where one can find the material that is too expensive for the ordinary person to buy, or too complex to find online. Such facilities are worth funding publicly because the return in informed citizenship and civic pride is far in excess of the money spent.

Libraries also have that undervalued resource—the trained librarian. The ultimate
40 Achilles' heel of the internet is that it presents every page of information as being

equally valid, which is of course nonsense. The internet is cluttered with false information, or just plain junk. The library, with its collection honed and developed by experts, is a guarantee of the quality and veracity of the information contained therein, something that Google can never provide.

45 Libraries have another function still, which the internet cannot fulfil. Libraries, like museums, are custodians of knowledge—and should be funded as such. It has become the fashion in recent decades to turn our great national libraries and museums into entertainment centres, with audio-visuals, interactive displays and gimmicks. While I have some enthusiasm for popularising esoteric knowledge, it cannot always be reduced

50 to the level of a child's view of the universe. We have a duty to future generations to invest in the custodians of our culture, in particular its literature and manuscripts.

Of course, I can't wait for Google to get online with the Bodleian Library's one million books. Yet here's one other thing I learned from a physical library space: the daunting scale of human knowledge and our inability to truly comprehend even a fraction of

55 it. On arriving at Glasgow University library, I did a quick calculation of how many economics books there were on the shelves and realised that I could not read them all. Ever. From which realisation comes the beginning of wisdom—and that is very different from merely imbibing information.

PASSAGE 2

In the second passage Ben Macintyre, writing in The Times newspaper, also in December 2004, responds to the same news, and considers the future of the "traditional library".

PARADISE IS PAPER, PARCHMENT AND DUST

I have a halcyon library memory. I am sitting under a cherry tree in the tiny central courtyard of the Cambridge University Library, a book in one hand and an almond slice in the other. On the grass beside me is an incredibly pretty girl. We are surrounded by eight million books. Behind the walls on every side of the courtyard, the books stretch

5 away in compact ranks hundreds of yards deep, the shelves extending at the rate of two miles a year. There are books beneath us in the subterranean stacks, and they reach into the sky; we are entombed in words, an unimaginable volume of collected knowledge in cold storage, quiet and vast and waiting.

Perhaps that was the moment I fell in love with libraries.

10 Or perhaps it was earlier, growing up in Scotland, when the mobile library would lurch up the road with stocks of Enid Blyton for the kids and supplies of bodice-rippers on the top shelf with saucy covers, to be giggled over when the driver-librarian was having his cup of tea.

Or perhaps the moment came earlier yet, when my father took me deep into the Bodleian

15 in Oxford and I inhaled, for the first time, that intoxicating mixture of paper, parchment and dust.

I have spent a substantial portion of my life since in libraries, and I still enter them with a mixture of excitement and awe. I am not alone in this. Veneration for libraries is as old as writing itself, for a library is more to our culture than a collection of books: it is

20 a temple, a symbol of power, the hushed core of civilisation, the citadel of memory, with its own mystique, social and sensual as well as intellectual.

But now a revolution, widely compared to the invention of printing itself, is taking place among the book shelves, and the library will never be the same again. This week Google announced plans to digitise fifteen million books from five great libraries,
25 including the Bodleian.

Some fear that this total library, vast and invisible, could finally destroy traditional libraries, which will become mere warehouses for the physical objects, empty of people and life. However, the advantages of a single scholarly online catalogue are incalculable and rather than destroying libraries, the internet will protect the written word as
30 never before, and render knowledge genuinely democratic. Fanatics always attack the libraries first, dictators seek to control the literature, elites hoard the knowledge that is power. Shi Huangdi, the Chinese emperor of the 3rd century BC, ordered that all literature, history and philosophy written before the founding of his dynasty should be destroyed. More books were burnt in the 20th century than any other—in Nazi
35 Germany, Bosnia and Afghanistan. With the online library, the books will finally be safe, and the bibliophobes will have been beaten, for ever.

But will we bother to browse the shelves when we can merely summon up any book in the world with the push of a button? Are the days of the library as a social organism over? Almost certainly not, for reasons psychological and, ultimately, spiritual. Locating a
40 book online is one thing, reading it is quite another, for there is no aesthetic substitute for the physical object; the computer revolution rolls on inexorably, but the world is reading more paper books than ever.

And the traditional library will also survive, because a library is central to our understanding of what it is to be human. Libraries are not just for reading in, but
45 for sociable thinking, exploring and exchanging ideas. They were never silent. Technology will not change that, for even in the starchiest heyday of Victorian self-improvement, libraries were intended to be meeting places of the mind, recreational as well as educational. The Openshaw branch of the Manchester public library was built complete with a billiard room. Of course just as bookshops have become trendy,
50 offering brain food and cappuccinos, so libraries, under financial and cultural pressure, will have to evolve by more actively welcoming people in to wander and explore . . . and fall in love.

Bookish types have always feared change and technology, but the book, and the library, have adapted and endured, retaining their essential magic. Even Hollywood understood.
55 In the 1957 film Desk Set, Katherine Hepburn plays a librarian-researcher whose job is threatened by a computer expert (Spencer Tracy) introducing new technology. In the end, the computer turns out to be an asset, not a danger, Tracy and Hepburn end up smooching, and everyone reads happily ever after.

The marriage of Google and the Bodleian will surely be the same.

[END OF SPECIMEN QUESTION PAPER]

[C270/SQP273]

English	Time: 1 hour 45 minutes	NATIONAL
Higher		QUALIFICATIONS
Close Reading—Questions		
Specimen Question Paper		

Answer all questions.

50 marks are allocated to this paper.

A code letter (U, A, E) is used alongside each question to give some indication of the skills being assessed. The number of marks attached to each question will give some indication of the length of answer required.

When answering questions coded "U—Understanding", use your own words as far as is reasonably possible and do not simply repeat the wording of the passage.

Questions on Passage 1   *Marks   Code*

> *You are reminded of the instruction on the front cover:*
> When answering questions coded "U—Understanding", use your own words as far as is reasonably possible and do not simply repeat the wording of the passage.

1. Read lines 1–6.

    (a)   What two contrasting emotions does the writer have about the plan to put the great university libraries online?   2   U

    (b)   How does the writer's word choice in these lines help to convey his view of the importance of "physical libraries" (line 5)? Refer to **two** examples in your answer.   2   A

2. In your opinion, does the writer think Glasgow Council gave the library in Drumchapel a high priority? Justify your answer by close reference to lines 7–13.   2   U/E

3. Show how the writer uses imagery **and** word choice in lines 14–22 to convey the "wonder of the library as a physical space".   4   A

4. Read lines 23–32.

    (a)   Show how the writer's language in lines 23–27 conveys his attitude to the "MTV generation". You should refer in your answer to such features as sentence structure, word choice, tone . . .   3   A

    (b)   Explain the "downward spiral" (line 32) to which the writer refers.   1   U

5. (a)   Give **four** reasons the writer presents in lines 33–44 in favour of maintaining traditional public libraries.   4   U

    (b)   Show how the writer's word choice in lines 39–44 emphasises the contrast between his attitude to libraries and his attitude to the internet.   2   A

6. Read lines 45–51.

    (a)   Twice in this paragraph the writer refers to libraries as "custodians". What does this word mean?   1   U

    (b)   Show how the language of lines 45–51 suggests that the writer has some reservations about the entertainment aspect of present day libraries and museums.   2   A

7. How effective do you find the ideas and/or language of the final paragraph (lines 52–58) as a conclusion to the passage as a whole?   3   E

                                                                            (26)

Questions on Passage 2   *Marks   Code*

You are reminded of the instruction on the front cover:
When answering questions coded "U—Understanding", use your own words as far as is reasonably possible and do not simply repeat the wording of the passage.

---

8. Read lines 1–16.

    (*a*)   Briefly describe the mood created in lines 1–3 ("I have . . . girl.").   **1**   **U**

    (*b*)   Show how the writer's use of language in lines 3–8 ("We are . . . waiting.") conveys a sense of awe.   **3**   **A**

    (*c*)   How effective do you find the repetition of "perhaps" (lines 9–16) in conveying the writer's recollections about libraries?   **2**   **A/E**

9. By referring to one example, show how the writer's imagery in lines 17–21 conveys the importance of libraries.   **2**   **A**

10. Read lines 22–36.

    Explain:

    (*a*)   what, according to the writer, the potential disadvantage of the online library is;   **1**   **U**

    (*b*)   what, according to the writer, the advantages of the online library are.   **3**   **U**

11. Read lines 37–52.

    (*a*)   Explain what the writer means by "there is no aesthetic substitute for the physical object" (lines 40–41).   **2**   **U**

    (*b*)   Explain why the writer believes libraries will "survive" (line 43).   **2**   **U**

12. How effectively does the writer use the reference to the film Desk Set to conclude the passage in a pleasing way? Refer in your answer to the ideas and language of lines 53–59.   **3**   **E**

                                                                    (19)

Question on both Passages

13. Consider the attitude displayed by each writer to traditional libraries (ie the type we have at the moment as opposed to an online library).

    Referring to important ideas in the passages, identify the key areas on which they agree.

    You may answer this question in continuous prose or in a series of developed bullet points.   **5**   **U/E**

                                                                    (5)

            [*END OF SPECIMEN QUESTION PAPER*]   **Total (50)**

[BLANK PAGE]

X270/12/02

NATIONAL
QUALIFICATIONS
2012

THURSDAY, 17 MAY
11.05AM – 12.35 PM

ENGLISH
HIGHER
Critical Essay

Answer **two** questions.

Each question must be taken from a different section.

Each question is worth 25 marks.

Answer TWO questions from this paper. Each question must be chosen from a different Section (A–E). You are not allowed to choose two questions from the same Section.

In all Sections you may use Scottish texts.

Write the number of each question in the margin of your answer booklet and begin each essay on a fresh page.

You should spend about 45 minutes on each essay.

The following will be assessed:

- the relevance of your essays to the questions you have chosen, and the extent to which you sustain an appropriate line of thought

- your knowledge and understanding of key elements, central concerns and significant details of the chosen texts, supported by detailed and relevant evidence

- your understanding, as appropriate to the questions chosen, of how relevant aspects of structure/style/language contribute to the meaning/effect/impact of the chosen texts, supported by detailed and relevant evidence

- your evaluation, as appropriate to the questions chosen, of the effectiveness of the chosen texts, supported by detailed and relevant evidence

- the quality of your written expression and the technical accuracy of your writing.

SECTION A—DRAMA

Answers to questions on drama should address relevantly the central concern(s)/theme(s) of the text and be supported by reference to appropriate dramatic techniques such as: conflict, characterisation, key scene(s), dialogue, climax, exposition, dénouement, structure, plot, setting, aspects of staging (such as lighting, music, stage set, stage directions . . .), soliloquy, monologue . . .

1. Choose a play in which a character shows signs of instability at one or more than one key point in the play.

    Explain the reason(s) for the character's instability and discuss how this feature adds to your understanding of the central concern(s) of the play.

2. Choose a play in which an important part is played by one of the following: crime, punishment, retribution.

    Show how the dramatist explores the issue and discuss its importance to your understanding of character and/or theme in the play as a whole.

3. Choose from a play a scene which you find amusing or moving or disturbing.

    Explain how the scene provokes this response and discuss how this aspect of the scene contributes to your understanding of the play as a whole.

4. Choose a play in which a central character's changing view of himself/herself is an important feature.

    Show how the dramatist makes you aware of the character's changing view of himself/herself and discuss how this affects your understanding of the character in the play as a whole.

SECTION B—PROSE

Prose Fiction

> *Answers to questions on prose fiction should address relevantly the central concern(s)/theme(s) of the text(s) and be supported by reference to appropriate techniques of prose fiction such as: characterisation, setting, key incident(s), narrative technique, symbolism, structure, climax, plot, atmosphere, dialogue, imagery . . .*

5. Choose a **novel** or **short story** which explores loss or futility or failure.

   Discuss how the writer explores one of these ideas in a way you find effective.

6. Choose a **novel** in which a main character refuses to accept advice or to conform to expectations.

   Explain the circumstances of the refusal and discuss its importance to your understanding of the character in the novel as a whole.

7. Choose a **novel** in which a particular mood is dominant.

   Explain how the novelist creates this mood and discuss how it contributes to your appreciation of the novel as a whole.

8. Choose a **novel** or **short story** in which there is a character who is not only realistic as a person but who has symbolic significance in the text as a whole.

   Show how the writer makes you aware of both aspects of the character.

Prose Non-fiction

> *Answers to questions on prose non-fiction should address relevantly the central concern(s)/theme(s) of the text and be supported by reference to appropriate techniques of prose non-fiction such as: ideas, use of evidence, selection of detail, point of view, stance, setting, anecdote, narrative voice, style, language, structure, organisation of material . . .*

9. Choose a **non-fiction text** which you consider to be a successful blend of narration and observation.

   Show how the writer successfully blends narration and observation, and discuss how this blend contributes to your appreciation of the text as a whole.

10. Choose a **non-fiction text** the conclusion of which you think is particularly effective.

    Explain why you find the conclusion to be so effective.

11. Choose a **non-fiction text** which engages you not only intellectually but also emotionally.

    Show how the writer successfully engages both your mind and your emotions.

SECTION C—POETRY

Answers to questions on poetry should address relevantly the central concern(s)/theme(s) of the text(s) and be supported by reference to appropriate poetic techniques such as: imagery, verse form, structure, mood, tone, sound, rhythm, rhyme, characterisation, contrast, setting, symbolism, word choice . . .

12. Choose a poem which features a complex character.

Show how the complexity of the character is presented and discuss how significant this aspect of characterisation is to the impact of the poem.

13. Choose a poem in which aspects of structure (such as verse form, rhyme, metre, repetition, climax, contrast, narrative development ...) play a significant role.

Show how the poet uses **at least two** structural features to enhance your appreciation of the poem as a whole.

14. Choose **two** poems which approach a similar theme in different ways.

Explain the nature of these different approaches and discuss which approach leads, in your opinion, to the more pleasing poem.

15. Choose a poem which explores **either** the problems of growing older **or** the joys of being young.

Show how the poet presents these aspects and discuss to what extent she/he succeeds in deepening your understanding of them.

SECTION D—FILM AND TV DRAMA

> *Answers to questions on film and TV drama should address relevantly the central concern(s)/ theme(s) of the text(s) and be supported by reference to appropriate techniques of film and TV drama such as: key sequence(s), characterisation, conflict, structure, plot, dialogue, editing/ montage, sound/soundtrack, aspects of mise-en-scène (such as lighting, colour, use of camera, costume, props . . .), mood, setting, casting, exploitation of genre . . .*

16. Choose a **film or TV drama*** which explores the experience of war.

   Show how the film or programme makers explore the experience and discuss to what extent they are successful in deepening your understanding of important aspects of war.

17. Choose a **film or TV drama*** in which symbolism is an important feature.

   Show how the film or programme makers create this symbolism and discuss its importance to your understanding of the text as a whole.

18. Choose a **film or TV drama*** set in a restricted environment such as an island, a ship, a prison, a hospital, a village, a house, a room . . .

   Show how the film or programme makers' use of this setting contributes to your understanding of character and theme.

19. Choose a **film or TV drama*** which explores a social, environmental or moral issue.

   Briefly explain the issue and go on to show how the film or programme makers explore it in a way you find effective.

*"TV Drama" includes a single play, a series or a serial.

SECTION E—LANGUAGE

Answers to questions on language should address relevantly the central concern(s) of the language research/study and be supported by reference to appropriate language concepts such as: register, jargon, tone, vocabulary, word choice, technical terminology, presentation, illustration, accent, grammar, idiom, slang, dialect, structure, point of view, orthography, abbreviation . . .

20. Consider some of the ways language is evolving as a result of advances in communication technology.

Basing your answer on specific examples, discuss to what extent these advances are improving or impeding communication.

21. Consider the spoken language of a particular geographical area.

Identify some of the characteristics of the language and discuss to what extent it enhances communication for the people of that area.

22. Consider the language of persuasion used in advertising or in politics.

Discuss several ways in which the language you have chosen attempts to be persuasive.

23. Consider aspects of language associated with a particular group in society which shares a professional or leisure activity.

Identify some examples of the language used and discuss how these examples facilitate communication within the group.

[END OF QUESTION PAPER]

[BLANK PAGE]

Acknowledgements

Permission has been sought from all relevant copyright holders and Bright Red Publishing is grateful for the use of the following:

Adapted extract taken from 'Shades of Green' by David Sinclair. Published by Grafton Books (Harper Collins). Reproduced with permission of David Sinclair (2008 Close Reading pages 2–3);

The article 'Yes, I will let Mr Prescott build in my backyard' by Richard Morrison © The Times/NI Syndication, 30 April 2004 (2008 Close Reading pages 3–4);

The article 'If Eco-Snobs had their way, none of us would go anywhere', by Janet Daley taken from The Telegraph © Telegraph Media Group Limited (8 January 2007) (2009 Close Reading pages 2–3);

The article 'Is it OK to fly?' by Leo Hickman, 20 May 2006. Copyright Guardian News & Media Ltd 2006 (2009 Close Reading pages 3–4).

The article 'Cities on the Edge of Chaos' by Deyan Sudjic, from The Observer, 9 March 2008. Copyright Guardian News & Media Ltd 2008 (2010 Close Reading pages 2–3);

An extract from 'The Dreaming City' by Gerry Hassan, Melissa Mean & Charlie Tims, 2007. Reproduced with permission of Demos (2010 Close Reading pages 3–4);

An extract from the article 'Want to exercise your mind? Try Playstation' by Steven Johnson © The Times/NI Syndication, 13 May 2005 (2011 Close Reading pages 2–3);

The article 'The Writing Is On The Wall' by Boris Johnson, taken from The Daily Telegraph © Telegraph Media Group Limited (28 December 2006) (2011 Close Reading pages 3–4);

An article adapted from 'Despite Google, we still need good libraries' by George Kerevan, taken from The Scotsman, 15 December 2004 © The Scotsman Publications Ltd. (2012 Close Reading pages 2–3);

The article 'Paradise is Paper, Vellum and Dust' by Ben Macintyre © The Times/NI Syndication, 18 December 2004 (2012 Close Reading pages 3–4).

SQA HIGHER ENGLISH
2008–2012

1. 1. gloss on "one could be forgiven for thinking that we still live in small peasant communities dependent upon the minutest shift in agricultural policy" – idea that we are still a rural society affected by farming laws or

2. gloss on "it has seemed almost as if we were still in the early nineteenth century when we relied on the countryside to survive" – as if we were still living in the past when we were more rurally dependent

2. (a) *Possible answers*:

Word choice:
1. "cried constantly":
   suggests a state of permanent outrage
2. "mortal danger" :
   suggests extreme peril, life-threatening
3. "greedy":
   suggests they are over-eager for monetary gain
4. "only motive is profit":
   suggests single-minded quest for gain
5. "kept on roaring":
   suggests persistent expression of anger, aggression
6. "killing every wild thing in sight": use of hyperbole to express scale of destruction
7. "threatening the very soil":
   intensive, emphasising extent of menace
8. "overuse":
   suggests injury by excessive use
9. "continually … ululating":
   suggests constant loud lamentations

Sentence structure:
10. listing (lines 12-14):
    emphasises the range of alternatives which provoke protest
11. repetition of "or":
    suggests determination to find a source of complaint
12. Tripartite structure of "One faction has cried", "another has kept on roaring" and "still another … ululating" in three sections separated by semi-colons building to a climax of noisy dissent.

(b) *Possible answers*:

Word choice:
1. "proliferation":
   suggests excessive increase in numbers
2. "dedicated":
   suggests obsessiveness, misplaced devotion
3. "multifarious":
   suggests an inappropriate or confusing variety
4. "have become accustomed":
   suggests force of habit rather than genuine concern
5. "expending":
   suggests consumption to little purpose
6. "their time and energies":
   suggests an all-consuming obsession
7. "countless other aspects":
   suggests needless involvement in every area

Sentence structure:
8. list of features (lines 15-16):
   range of objections conveys excessive nature of protests

9. list of projects (lines 18-20):
   excessive concern about a wide range of aspects of nature

Tone:
10. "moorlands, uplands, lowlands":
    dismissive tone – as if "any old lands"
11. any of 1-9 above could be discussed in terms of a dismissive, scathing, contemptuous tone

3. (a) 1. "returned to the central position" refers to the aim of the action groups mentioned in lines 15-20 (no credit for the quotation unless the reference back is identified)

2. "worrying aspect" points forward to concerns the writer has (no credit for the quotation unless the reference forward is identified)

(b) 1. acceptable gloss on "identification … of the countryside in general and the landscape in particular with the past", eg that rural features are the only way of understanding our history
2. desire to preserve what is perceived as "our heritage"
3. difficulty in defining what is meant by the term "our heritage"

4. (a) *Any two of the following*:
1. acceptable gloss on "our living link with our history" eg tangible, actual, real, visible connection with the past
2. acceptable gloss on "the visible expression of our British roots" eg outward display, evidence of our heritage, identity
3. failure to preserve the landscape will cause the connection to be lost

(b) *Any of the following*:
1. who we are by race, our sense of belonging, does not stem from the physical setting in which we live
2. there is no one connecting link between the countryside of today and the countryside of the past
3. many diverse influences have joined to create a landscape which has suited the creators' own purposes

(c) *Possible answers*:
1. "simply":
   pejorative, reductive view
2. *"as it is now"*:
   use of italics stresses the conservationists' total rejection of change
3. beginning sentence "Far from affirming history" emphasises mistaken approach
4. "affirming", "denies":
   juxtaposition of opposites reinforces the weakness of the conservationists' position
5. "actually": reinforces the contrast between affirmation and denial
6. "the continuous change without which history does not exist": final climactic assertion of writer's belief in direct opposition to the ideas of the conservationists

5. *Any three of the following*:
1. it is impossible to define a point in time for the start of "tradition"
2. conifers, which are unpopular nowadays, were significant in the past
3. our more iconic species of trees (oak and elm) arrived much later
4. animals (reindeer, rhinoceros, bison, hippopotamus, elephant) which have now vanished used to be abundant

5.   when man first appeared in Britain, the landscape was Arctic ice and tundra

6. (a) *Any two of the following*:
   1.   hunting became more difficult …
   2.   … as the grazing animals started to die out/became difficult to find …
   3.   … because of increased afforestation

   (b) *Any of the following*:
   1.   Stone Age man relied more on farming than on hunting
   2.   he improved the efficiency of his farming tools
   3.   he created space for grasslands for animals and/or crops
   4.   crops were increasingly grown to serve man's needs

7. (a) the middle classes are not really worried about the countryside; what really concerns them is: gloss on "(the threat to) their own pleasure" **or** on "(the threat to) the value of their own property"

   (b) *Possible answers*:
   1.   "heavy heart": deliberate exaggeration of the extent of his remorse
   2.   "class traitor": inflated description suggesting his opinions constitute some terrible act/betrayal
   3.   "middle-class, middle-aged property owner": writer deliberately casts himself as an archetype, clichéd representative of his class
   4.   "smugly watched": suggests the writer is complacent, self-satisfied, gloating
   5.   "soar in value":
        suggests a smug belief that his own success is both effortless and impressive
   6.   "inordinately proud":
        suggests a pride which is hard to justify, excessive, out of all proportion
   7.   "my view":
        suggests smug possessiveness
   8.   "from an upstairs window":
        lampoons/undercuts the writer's pride in his view by suggesting the view is limited, inaccessible, awkward…
   9.   "motorway flyover in between":
        suggests something man-made, ugly, functional – ridiculing the writer's pride in his view
   10. parenthesis (lines 7-8): apparently a throwaway qualification, but in reality used by the writer to highlight the overblown nature of his pride/undercut his argument
   11. repetition of "(And) I" at the start of sentences: suggests self-absorbed, egotistical, pompous nature of middle classes
   12. repetition of "I" followed by active verb: suggests an inflated belief in the importance of his actions/opinions
   13. contrast: the ghastliness of his self-satisfied pride ("smugly watched", "soar in value") is heightened by the contrast with the desperation of the "young househunters" (In developing this point some candidates might choose to comment on the balance of "more and more"/"fewer and fewer".)

8. *Possible answers*:

   Imagery:
   1.   "cherished credo":
        A "credo" is a religious belief. This suggests the reverence and/or depth of the middle classes" devotion to the countryside.
   2.   "forever sacrosanct":
        Something "sacrosanct" is sacred and untouchable. This implies an almost religious conviction that the countryside should remain unaltered, suggests the countryside is holy ground and changing it would be sacrilegious.

   3.   " 'Stalinist' decision": Stalin is considered to be an oppressive, ruthless dictator. This portrays the Government as dictatorial, evil, brutal, cruel, heartless …
   4.   "choked (by concrete)":
        Being "choked" involves strangulation, difficulty in breathing. This suggests the countryside is being destroyed, having the life squeezed out of it, unable to flourish, under attack.
   5.   "rapacious housebuilders":
        A "rapacious" act is a predatory one involving, for example, a bird of prey. This suggests the builders are aggressive, plundering, greedy, self-interested, voracious, gluttonous…
   6.   "devour whole landscapes":
        To "devour" something is to eat it up greedily. This suggests the builders are greedy, insatiable, all-consuming, indiscriminate…
   7.   "sprawling outward":
        To "sprawl" is to sit or lie in an awkward, ungainly way. This suggests the outward movement of the cities would be haphazard, unattractive, disorderly…
   8.   "will be swept away":
        "swept away" could refer to brushing or tidal movement. Either way, it suggests a rapid, extensive, conclusive end to the green belts.

   Word choice:
   9.   "verdant hills and dales":
        idealised, Eden-like vision of the countryside as lush, fertile
   10. "forever":
        intensifies belief in inviolable nature of the countryside
   11. "impose":
        suggests compulsion, force, authoritarian government
   12. "most hideous":
        superlatively repulsive, despicable, morally offensive
   13. "threat":
        suggests pain, injury, a menacing, bullying enemy…
   14. "our way of life":
        suggests a set of shared, traditional, important values
   15. "since the Luftwaffe … in 1940":
        (comparing the effect of more houses to the damage caused by German bombers) suggests they fear huge destruction, regard the builders as an evil, destructive, aggressive enemy
   16. "cherished green belts":
        the countryside is loved and treasured
   17. "14 great rings":
        majestic, impressive, powerful, important

   Register:
   18. candidates should be rewarded who make a sensible attempt to identify a register (inflated, over-the-top, exaggerated, mock-reverential, faux-outraged) and then – through appropriate reference and analysis – show how the writer's use of this register pokes fun at, attacks, exemplifies the views of the middle classes; any of the listed examples of imagery and word choice might be used to support such an answer

9. *Possible answers*:

   Sentence structure:
   1.   the positioning of "Yet" at the start of the opening sentence sets up the rebuttal of the preceding argument
   2.   contrast/balance in opening sentence of "sweep away"/"look at" moves argument forward
   3.   structure of opening sentence places emphasis on principal clause at its conclusion
   4.   short, (apparently) concessionary 2nd sentence, introduced by "Yes", is immediately qualified/contradicted by 3rd sentence

5. positioning of "But" at start of 3rd sentence sets up qualification/ contradiction to 2nd sentence
6. repetition of "seem crowded" following "crowded" also underlines 3rd sentence's qualification/contradiction
7. short, punchy, declarative final two sentences drive home writer's point
8. positioning of "Just" at start of final sentence underlines (surprisingly small) statistic
9. candidates may comment on the writer's general sign-posting at the start of sentences: "Yet", "Yes", "But", "Just" to flag up the oppositional nature of his argument

Word choice:
10. "sweep away":
    suggests previous argument is "rubbish" and can be dealt with/dismissed very quickly
11. "apoplectic":
    suggests uncontrolled, irrational anger
12. "froth":
    suggests something insubstantial, trivial…
13. "self-interested":
    suggests middle classes only concerned with themselves, not the countryside
14. "posturing":
    suggests middle classes" concern is exaggerated, contrived, fake, affected …
15. "look at the reality":
    suggests truth is clear and incontrovertible
16. "recedes dramatically":
    suggests rapid movement, significant diminution of threat
17. "overwhelmingly green":
    emphasises full extent of Britain's rural make-up
18. "classified":
    official nature of term reinforces accuracy, validity of statistic
19. use of personal pronouns ("you … we …us …our"): clear attempt to make the reader share his point of view/involve the reader personally

10. (a) 1. gloss on "wasteland, largely devoid of landscape beauty": eg it is a wilderness, it is not attractive, it serves no purpose, it has no redeeming features and
        2. there is a desperate shortage of housing in London (for reasons of space and/or cost)

(b) *Possible answers*:

Word choice
1. "myth":
   suggests belief is untrue, fictitious, irrational, fanciful
2. "Well, lungs they might be":
   suggests reluctant, grudging, conditional acceptance of claim
3. "not at all": definitive, categorical negative

Sentence structure:
4. "Well, lungs they might be":
   inversion places emphasis on writer's doubt/scepticism
5. "But":
   position at start of sentence introduces idea of rebuttal
6. parenthesis (line 30):
   used to point out slyly that the middle classes benefit commercially as well as environmentally
7. progressive nature of final sentence: using semi-colons, the writer divides final sentence into three sections to stress the diminishing benefits of green belts **and/or** the diminishing benefits are also signposted structurally by the use of "chiefly", "and then" and "and not at all" at the start of each section

8. climax of final sentence:
   writer uses colon to introduce, direct attention to those who are not advantaged by green belts

Tone:
9. "Well, lungs they might be":
   dismissive, sceptical tone stresses his lack of belief
10. "nice houses", "leafy suburbs":
    use of clichés creates a rather mocking tone towards those enjoying a comfortable, carefree existence
11. "(not least … values sky-high)": ironic aside underlines writer's scepticism towards middle classes

Other language features:
12. any other acceptable suggestion supported by appropriate reference and explanation

11. **First option (lines 33–37)**

(a) *Possible answer*:
    green-belt protectionists believe they are protecting land which has been unchanged for centuries when in reality each generation has changed the land as required

(b) *Possible answers*:

Word choice:
1. "claim":
   suggests doubt/dubiety
2. "rampant advance":
   suggests insatiable demands; uses hyperbole to make their claims seem absurd, over the top, fanciful
3. "bulldozers" (used to symbolise builders): connotations of indiscriminate destruction, demolition; again suggests protectionists' claims are deliberately exaggerated, alarmist
4. "exactly what":
   suggests claims lack detail
5. "imagine":
   suggests green-belt protectionists are removed from reality, living in a dream world
6. "Primordial forest", "Boadicea", "the Romans": deliberate reference to very distant times/people stresses the unlikeliness of the green-belt campaigners' claims **or** implicit comparison of their claims to Boadicea's heroic life-or-death battle against a genuine aggressor highlights their pretension, self-importance, lack of perspective
7. "Hogwash":
   categorical condemnation – claims are worthless, false, ridiculous, "garbage"
8. "making and remaking":
   suggests change is ongoing, inevitable process

Sentence structure:
9. repetition of questions: hectoring, nagging, confrontational
10. single-word sentence: highlights his utter rejection of their claims
11. fluent, formal final sentence (in comparison to previous sentence): controlled, certain, assured, rational

Tone:
12. scornful/dubious – "claim"
13. satirical – "rampant advance"
14. dismissive/incredulous – "exactly what", "imagine"
15. humorous – "primordial", "Boadicea thrashed the Romans"
16. dismissive, contemptuous – deliberate informality of "Hogwash"
17. authoritative, certain – created by formality of final sentence (in contrast to the previous sentence)

11. Second option (lines 38–43)

(a) *Possible answers*:

green-belt protectionists think the government is imposing change/being authoritarian but current planning laws are equally harsh/dictatorial **and/or** green-belt protectionists oppose the government's plans to build houses/change green belt planning but the existing planning laws have worked out poorly/been calamitous or are very protective of the countryside

(b) *Possible answers*:

Word choice:
1. "fond":
   suggests green-belt protectionists are self-indulgent, enjoy being critical
2. "deriding":
   suggests their arguments are cruel, contemptuous, destructive
3. "monstrous":
   deliberate exaggeration to make their claims seem excessive
4. "Soviet-style diktats":
   comparison to authoritarian state suggests green-belt protectionists' views are alarmist and excessive
5. "imagine":
   suggests their ideas are fanciful, unrealistic…
6. "disastrous":
   suggests horrific, life-threatening, widespread effects of existing laws
7. "impact":
   suggests powerful, negative, destructive force of existing laws

Sentence structure:
8. "Good grief":
   positioning at start of sentence establishes exasperated tone of diatribe to follow
9. "…and often disastrous,":
   adds additional layer of criticism
10. rhetorical question:
    stylistic device inviting reader to share the writer's beliefs
11. "not just … but":
    this construction allows the writer to expand his argument into other areas, build his argument to a climax
12. listing "on … on …on":
    repetitive structure suggests scale, variety of problems caused by current laws

Tone:
13. scornful – "fond"
14. satirical – "monstrous, Soviet-style diktats"
15. exasperated, frustrated, angry, incredulous – "Good grief", "what on earth do they imagine"
16. passionate, increasingly angry – "on employment … on economic growth?"

12. *Possible answers*

Ideas:
1. writer brings argument back to shortage of housing – a key issue introduced in the opening paragraph and referred to throughout the passage
2. writer focuses again on the selfishness, aggression, insularity, idealised views of the middle classes – themes discussed at various points throughout the passage.

3. writer looks at those affected ("young and poor") by the middle classes' campaigns and the problems they have (lack of housing, inability to advance themselves, long distances to travel to work) – attempting to damn the middle classes' opposition.

Style:
4. "And … on homelessness":
   link to or climax of argument from previous paragraph, returning argument to its primary concern
5. "homelessness":
   somewhat sensationalised term, a deliberate (and misleading?) attempt by the writer to evoke our sympathy
6. "Every time":
   wearisome inevitability of middle class campaigning
7. "bunch":
   suggests a gang or a loose grouping lacking authority or credibility; derogatory term continues criticism of middle classes
8. "fights off":
   criticism of middle classes' combative, aggressive stance
9. " 'intrusion' ":
   use of inverted commas reiterates misguided nature of middle class objections
10. "cherished landscape":
    satirical tone, once again poking fun at the middle classes" idealised, possessive vision of the countryside
11. "young and poor":
    attempt to tug at the readers' heartstrings and emphasise the cruelty of the middle classes' opposition
12. "reasonable proximity", "somewhere to live":
    the reasonable, understated goals of those seeking houses stand in contrast to the middle classes' unyielding, isolationist, unhelpful position
13. "pulling up drawbridge … castle": extended metaphor again suggests the insular/selfish, feudal, old-fashioned, elitist, uncaring, NIMBYist nature of the middle classes.

Question on both Passages

13. The mark for this question should reflect the overall quality of the response and may not be directly related to the length of the response or to the number of points/reference made. A succinct sophisticated response should be worth more than a series of fairly trivial points and obvious references.

For full marks there must be reference to both passages (although not necessarily a balanced treatment) and convincing evaluative comment.

Any of the points below would be valid comment:

Passage 1

Ideas
- surprise that there is such wide coverage of the countryside debate
- balance of ideas both past and present day
- awareness of the wide extent of claims put forward by conservationists
- strong feelings of those who feel the countryside is under threat
- writer's disapproval of action groups
- conservationists' view of our national identity is discredited
- concept of our national identity and the complexities involved
- history requires "continuous change"
- difficulties in establishing the "traditional British landscape"
- the landscape is determined by human influence not the environment

Style
- impersonal
- language used to highlight the strong feelings of conservationists: "so extensive …", "so fierce the passions …"
- repetition of "so"
- mocking tone
- word choice focusing on alleged dangers to the countryside: "mortal danger", "threatening", "killing", "overuse of machinery"
- tone of disapproval
- word choice to discredit claims: "It might be thought", "widely assumed", "assumptions", "wildly overused term is seriously misleading"
- the short sentence to refute the claims: "This view is palpably nonsensical."
- imagery such as: "single thread", "bewildering array"
- balance of past/present
- impact of title/headline

Passage 2

Ideas
- the hypocrisy of the English middle classes regarding the countryside
- extreme nature of their view of the threat to the countryside
- the threat is much less serious than has been suggested
- some of the green belt around London should be used for housing
- the theory about green belts as "lungs" is a myth
- the flawed arguments of the "green-belt protectionists"
- green belts benefit property owners not those on inner city estates
- middle class homeowners react to any encroachment on their land and this makes it more difficult for the young and the poor to find suitable housing

Style
- personal involvement of the writer
- self-mocking tone regarding his own middle class position
- word choice to show extreme nature of the alleged threat to the countryside: "choked by concrete", "rapacious housebuilders"
- imagery in lines 11-19
- statistics in lines 20-24
- imagery in lines 25-32
- one-word sentence to dismiss claims made by conservationists: "Hogwash."
- conclusion: imagery of castle, drawbridge, …
- impact of title/headline

ENGLISH HIGHER CRITICAL ESSAY 2008

Please see the Critical Essay guidelines for the English Higher 2012 on page 117.

ENGLISH HIGHER
CLOSE READING 2009

1. (a) *Any two of the following*:

Acceptable gloss on/understanding of:

1. "absence of world war"	there is no world war/global conflict (to make travel difficult, dangerous)
2. "(unprecedented) prosperity"	people are well-off, wealthy (as never before)
3. "just as working people … generations"	travel has become democratic, available to all, no longer the sole preserve of the rich
4. "enjoy"	travel is fun, pleasurable, …
5. "other cultures … other climates"	travel allows people to experience different ways of life
6. "liberating possibilities"	travel broadens the mind, gives people greater insights into the world

(b) *Possible answers are*:

Sentence structure:

1. use of questions	first question is what politicians are asking the public to consider; second question shows the writer's incredulous response/immediate opposition **and/or** a case might be made that the repetition of the questions and/or the use of questions to open the passage indicates the combative, populist, anti-restriction stance of the writer
2. use of parenthesis in first paragraph ("the experience … climates")	to identify/exemplify the benefits/ freedoms of travel
3. use of list ("other cultures … climates")	to identify/exemplify the multiplicity of these benefits
4. repetition of "other"	to emphasise the multiplicity/variety of the experiences travel affords and/or to emphasise the very different nature of other countries
5. balanced structure of the "Just as … their reach" sentence	describing the many benefits of air travel in the first half of the sentence makes the negative thrust of its conclusion all the more forceful
6. use of "And" at start of second paragraph	unusual placement of conjunction is an eye-catching, forceful indication of the start of her personal opposition
7. use of parenthesis in second paragraph ("most of them comfortably off")	(rather sneering aside) to remind us that politicians are part of the rich elite who will still be able to travel/be unaffected by the restrictions
8. balanced structure/contrast of the "Maybe Tommy … social revelation" sentence	the writer concedes that there is a negative aspect to the democratisation of travel but shows the relative unimportance of this in the second half of the sentence via her sweeping affirmation of the large-scale benefits of travel

Word choice:	
9. "freedoms"	suggests that travel offers people independence, broadens their horizons, …
10. "experience"	suggests something life-enhancing
11. "liberating (possibilities)"	suggests that travel allows people a freer, less constrained life-style
12. "enlightenment"	suggests travel can result in a fundamental increase/transformation in people's knowledge or happiness
13. "pleasure"	suggests enjoyment, gratification, …
14. "(I reach for my) megaphone"	suggests strident, highly vocal, intense, I'm-standing-on-a-soapbox-and-you'd-better-listen opposition
15. "thousands (of people)"	suggests sheer number who have benefited from travel
16. "(would never have) ventured"	suggests limited nature of parents' experience as compared with current possibilities
17. "(social) revelation"	suggests life-changing benefit

2. *Four elements are required*:

   1. "eco-lobby's anti-flying agenda" …

   2. … refers back to the restrictive air travel proposals discussed in the opening two paragraphs;

   3. "their strategy as a whole"/"can we just review"

   4. … leads into the discussion of the eco-lobby's proposed restrictions on travel as a whole/on energy use in general

3. (*a*) acceptable gloss on "creates intolerable pressure on the others" eg it puts (unbearable) stresses and strains on other forms of transport

   (*b*) The nub of the answer lies in the information in lines 21-23: the congestion charge discouraged many commuters from driving into London and as a result London's train and tube services are now intolerably busy/putting prices up to reduce numbers.

4. (*a*) *Either or both of the following*:

   1. mobility allows people to come together for a variety of beneficial reasons – for work, for pleasure and for people from different backgrounds to share knowledge/understand one another better (for full marks for this point alone, candidates will have to show reasonable understanding of "social/professional/cultural interactions")

   2. many shared activities – which are only possible thanks to mobility – have made cities vital in the advancement of learning (for full marks for this point alone, candidates will have to show reasonable understanding of "centres of intellectual progress")

   (*b*) Some candidates may identify a negative tone (angry, scathing, dismissive, sarcastic, caustic …) or they may just assume the tone is one of "disapproval". Some candidates, however, may focus on the more positive, celebratory tone adopted by the writer in the second half of the paragraph which also conveys her disapproval of the anti-mobility "solution".

   Possible answers are:

1. "and I am just waiting"	suggests writer's world-weary mistrust of politicians and the inevitability of their actions
2. "none/anywhere"	emphasising the extreme nature of the "solution"
3. "craven retreat"	suggests the "solution" would be a cowardly, unworthy, retrograde step
4. "Renaissance"	positive reference to a very enlightened, progressive, civilised period
5. "intellectual progress"	suggests society/civilisation moving forward in very considered, enlightened manner
6. parenthesis ("and I am … explicitly")	knowing aside to the readers about the bandwagon-joining propensities of politicians
7. "Stay at home and save the planet."	this parody of facile, instant sloganeering shows the writer's contempt for the quick-fix solutions of the eco-lobby
8. "social, professional and cultural"	accumulated list of benefits made possible by mobility
9. structure of the final sentence	the positioning (and the bluntness) of "But that" presages her explicit rejection of the "solution" **and/or** the dash (followed by "and") is used to introduce an additional point to the argument, effectively building the sentence to a resonant, powerful, pro-mobility climax

5. (*a*) Candidates need to show a basic understanding of "you'd still be making liberal use of the technology that has transformed domestic life": eg people would still use a lot of energy in their houses.

   (*b*) *The following three key ideas for 1 mark each:*

   1. (heating) has reduced/nearly eradicated certain (respiratory) diseases

   2. (hot water/more effective cleaning) reduced/nearly eradicated disease-carrying pests/parasites/insects

   3. (the car) has given people independence, broadened their horizons, made it easier for people to move about ("freedom")
   or (the car) has allowed people to be much more adaptable/less rigid, to have more choice in their lives ("flexibility")

(c) *Possible answers are*:

1. repetition of "Never mind …"	stresses her vehement, outraged opposition to so many of the restrictive measures (described previously) **and/or** the cumulative effect of having three sentences all starting with "Never mind" shows that she is opposed to the eco-lobby for a variety of reasons/on a variety of fronts
2. repetition in "the very young and the very old"	stresses that it is the most vulnerable members of society who would be put most at risk by such restrictions
3. parenthesis (dashes)	allows her to name two particularly frightening/dangerous diseases, thus underlining the vital importance of heating/extreme dangers in cutting down on heating
4. parenthesis (brackets)	allows her to show the horrific threat posed by these pests, "plague" being associated with widespread, uncontrollable death
5. parenthesis (commas)	the insertion of "Green Public Enemy Number One" allows the writer to slip in a satirical jab at (what she perceives as) the silly, over-the-top scaremongering of the eco-lobby

(d) It would bring back a very divided society, a society split into rich and poor, a society of haves and have-nots ("reconstructing a class divide") which would be very bad/disastrous/detrimental to the poor, the have-nots, the less fortunate, the disadvantaged.

6. (a) Any acceptable gloss, eg (a hypothesis that suggests) the end of the world, global disaster, human annihilation, …

(b) *The following two points for 1 mark each*:

1. it would not be possible to grow enough food to deal with the world's ever-increasing population

2. the only things which would prevent large-scale starvation would be comparably terrible events.

(c) *Any two of the following points*
Acceptable gloss on/understanding of:

1. "complexity of human behaviour"	people don't always conform to a pattern, behave as expected
2. "Population…responded to economic and social conditions"	the rate of population growth was determined by people's environment/ particular circumstances
3. "force of ingenuity", "inventiveness and innovation"	people were smarter/more resourceful than he imagined
4. "intensive farming … invention of pesticides …"	new farming methods and scientific advances dramatically increased the amount of food
5. "simple, fixed relation between numbers of people and amount of resource"	his basic assumptions were wrong: the ratio of people to food became more complex than he had imagined

7. *The following points could be made*:

1. "Warnings of catastrophe come and go"	suggests such warnings are transient, unimportant, not unusual; not worthy of the current over-reaction (a case might be made that the shortness of this sentence suggests a blunt, unequivocal dismissal on the writer's part)
2. "Whatever their validity"	suggests writer's scepticism
3. "we cannot and should not"	rhetorical repetition and cadence to emphasise, assertive, decisive opposition
4. "more restricted way of life"	suggests loss of freedom
5. "anyway"	dismissive tone, rejecting underlying concept of restrictions
6. "impracticable"	highlights fundamental flaws in the proposals
7. "grotesquely unfair"	suggests a monstrous, outlandish travesty of justice
8 "socially divisive"	suggests an attack on the very fabric of society
9. repetition of the "If" structure in the final two sentences	could be argued that this brings the passage to a climax: the penultimate sentence an emphatic summing-up of her objections, the final sentence an affirmation of her belief in human resourcefulness

7. *continued*

10. repetition of "we" throughout paragraph	suggests writer is taking a stand for all of us; underlines her belief that this is something we can solve together as opposed to being dictated to by government
11. general use of pairs as a rhetorical device: "cannot and should not", "grotesquely unfair and socially divisive", "'innovate and engineer"	candidates may find the repetitive use of this device gives the paragraph a persuasive certainty. On the other hand, they may find it somewhat repetitive, wearisome, contrived, mechanical, …

8. (*a*) *Answers should show an understanding of*:

"how to square this urge… responsible citizen" eg the writer loves travelling/wants to fly but also wants to act sensibly/do the right thing/be free of guilt.

(*b*) *Possible answers are*:

Word choice:

1. "I", "my"	suggests the personal impact on his life
2. "desperate"	exaggerated sense of urgency, panic, distress
3. "loved"	suggests strong/deep personal attachment
4. "descended"	indicates the downward turn his life has taken
5. "near-permanent depression"	exaggerates dire consequences
6. "young (daughters)"	slightly manipulative reference to the young as innocent/vulnerable/representatives of future generations
7. "abstinence"	implies a sense of personal sacrifice

Sentence structure:

8. "Please someone…"	exaggerated sense of direct plea to anyone; (mock) melodramatic
9. rhetorical question "who doesn't ?"	to justify his argument by implying that his love of travel applies to everybody
10. parenthetical "and … young daughters"	sets himself up as caring family man; drives home extent of implications
11. use of questions	to highlight uncertainty/insecurity
12. repetition of "I", "my"	as point 1
Use of contrast:	
13. "at least"/"at best"	use of superlatives to highlight ultimate scenarios

Use of contrast:

13. "at least"/"at best"	use of superlatives to highlight ultimate scenarios

9. (*a*) There must be some indication that the candidate understands the term "irony". A "two-pronged" answer is required, in candidate's own words as far as possible.
The key point is that the conference is connected to "how damaging" flying is to the environment, yet delegates have "flown from around the world" to be there.

(*b*) *Possible answers are*:

Sentence structure:

1. repetition ("speaker after speaker")	to emphasise the sheer number of delegates of like mind, claiming victimisation of the industry …
2. use of colon	to introduce so-called justification for their case by singling out what they claim are even greater causes of pollution
3. use of questions in the final two sentences	designed to divert attention from their culpability

9. (b) *continued*

Word choice:

4. "bemoaned", "cried"	use of negative language to emphasise the self-pitying, whingeing nature of the delegates
5. "somehow"	suggests it has happened by chance/not based on logic
6. "…in perspective"	assumed rationality followed by obfuscation
7. "singled out", "chase after", "picking on"	presenting themselves as harassed victims
8. "efficiency savings"	delegates' euphemism to disguise effects on other industries
9. "gives so much to the world"	sanctimonious self-justification
10. "economically fragile"	supposed claims of being delicate, vulnerable, frail, …

Tone:

11. mocking, satirical, pejorative, belittling …	supported by sensible comment such as: - the use of reported speech (eg "Why … singled out?") to replicate sound of whingeing complaints - presentation of themselves as victimised underdogs - colloquial language ("small fry", "singled out", "chase after", "picking on") to present delegates as juvenile, shallow - "they cried … they said" creates sense of constant complaint … - or appropriate comment using any of points 1-10 above

(c) *Possible answers/comments are*:

1. "etched (over one another)".	just as etching involves cutting into a surface, using acid or a sharp implement, so the Earth will be permanently damaged by a crisscrossing indentation of flightpaths	2. "scarred"	just as a scar is a mark left by a wound, there will be permanent disfigurement to the Earth

10. *A gloss of the key points in lines 31-33 for 1 mark each, ie*:

1. to offset environmental cost ("the polluter must pay")

2. to reduce numbers of people flying ("to drive down demand")

11. *Possible answers are*:

1. "nice cuddly idea"	suggests something childish, spuriously comforting **and/or** use of colloquial language is incongruous when juxtaposed with scientific terminology beforehand
2. "on the surface"	suggests superficial thinking
3. references to Thailand and Honduras	selection of worthy activities/distant locations to convey relatively low-impact options
4. "handing out"	suggests a mere distribution exercise, an easy option, something rather patronising
5. "job done"	flippancy of short-term fix idea
6. "(simply) carry on flying"	clichéd, complacent attitude of those indifferent to looking for remedies
7. "regardless"	the last word in passage highlights irresponsibility

Question on both Passages

12. The mark for this question should reflect the overall quality of the response and may not be directly related to the length of response or to the number of points/references made. A succinct, sophisticated response should be worth more than a series of fairly trivial points and obvious references.

For full marks there must be a reference to both elements (ie ideas and style) and to both passages (although not necessarily a balanced treatment) and convincing evaluative comment.

Ideas – Passage 1:
- to save limited natural resources, threat of restrictions to freedom to travel
- opportunities to experience new places being denied
- advantages of air travel as "a social revelation"
- green taxes affect London road transport and rail fares, as well as air travel
- importance of travel to allow social, professional and cultural interaction
- proposed restrictions on scarce resources would also extend to our homes
- benefits of modern technology in preventing disease and providing freedom
- reconstruction of a new class divide would result from politicians' environmental restrictions
- possibility of mortal danger from global warming
- dire environmental warnings from the past have not been realised
- instead of unfair restrictions, we must devise a method of managing the predicted environmental crisis

Ideas – Passage 2
- conflict between desire to fly and duty to be a responsible citizen
- concern for the future and necessity of restricting flying
- map evidence of extent of current flightpaths
- presentation of stark choice between status quo or cutting back on air travel
- personal view that flying must become more expensive to reduce demand
- other remedies to offset the damage would merely mask the continuing problem caused by flying

Style – Passage 1
- use of questions to stimulate debate
- use of passionate language to convey strength of feeling about restricted travel
- introduction of exaggerated illustration
- reasoned debating style
- use of London congestion charge as an illustration
- use of a disapproving tone to ridicule proposed travel restrictions
- rhetorical, exhortatory repetition to convey view that removal of modern advances would be ludicrous
- introduction of historical example

Style – Passage 2
- use of conversational tone
- use of personal anecdote
- use of others' views to convey misconceptions about the damage caused by air travel
- introduction of emotionally charged comment to convey strength of feeling
- use of questions to convey the alternative sides of the debate

ENGLISH HIGHER CRITICAL ESSAY 2009

Please see the Critical Essay guidelines for the English Higher 2012 on page 117.

ENGLISH HIGHER
CLOSE READING 2010

Questions on Passage 1

1. (*a*) *There must be some attempt to use own words.*
   Gloss on the following two terms for:

"the dispossessed"	people who are homeless, displaced, driven from their own land, alienated from their own society, poor people, people with few possessions
"the ambitious"	people with a strong desire to succeed, to get on in life, to better themselves, to make money

   (*b*) *Marks will depend on the quality of comment on the chosen words. For full marks, two examples must be dealt with.*
   Possible answers are:

1. "flooding into"	suggests a force which is powerful, massive, unstoppable, out of control, coming at great speed, impossible to contain, …
2. "swollen"	suggests something bloated, unnatural, disfigured, …
3. "out of all recognition"	suggests essential nature of the cities has been massively altered, ruined, compromised, …
4. "struggling (to cope)"	suggests dealing with this influx is difficult, challenging, a battle, …
5. "reconfiguring"	suggests fundamental change
6. "at breakneck speed"	suggests speed of change involved is reckless, dangerously fast, likely to lead to disaster, …
7. "(industrial) powerhouse"	suggests something very forceful, strong, energetic has been created **or** suggests something which will make a great impact on, influence, benefit, dominate its surroundings

2. *There must be some attempt to "explain".*
   The following points for both marks:
   1. officially, London is now a city of almost 8 million **and/or** in reality, London is now a city of 18 million, much larger than the "version" referred to (which had a population of two million)
   2. (because it is now spread over a vast area) London is more sprawling, less definable, less cohesive than the "version" referred to.

3. *Marks will depend on the quality of comment. Insightful comment on one feature could be worth up to 3 marks. For full marks, there must be reference to more than one feature.*
   When dealing with imagery, answers must show recognition of the literal root of the image and then explore how the writer is extending it figuratively.
   Candidates may well choose to deal with the points listed here under "Imagery" as word choice.
   Possible answers are:
   Imagery:

1. "reeled back"	"to reel" is to stagger, sway or recoil, from the impact of a blow or in shock or disbelief. This suggests a deep-seated, almost physical revulsion, a desire to step back from what they found, a sense of them losing control and being shaken to their very foundations
2. "(hideous) tumour"	a tumour is a growth or a mass of diseased cells which can lead to serious illness or death. This suggests the Victorians felt that London was unhealthy, malignant, evil, increasingly invasive, destructive to the country as a whole
3. "sucking the life out of"	the comparison here is with a blood-sucking creature (or even a vampire). This suggests the Victorians felt that London was essentially parasitic, feeding off and likely to damage or destroy the countryside, while having no positive value of its own

Word choice:

4. "in horror"	shows their deep-seated shock and fear
5. "cholera-ridden"	disease was dominant, pervasive, deep-seated, …
6. "hideous (tumour)"	London was deeply unpleasant, repellent, ghastly, …
7. "polluted"	they felt the city was unwholesome, impure, contaminated, …
8. "squalor"	they felt the city was sordid, dirty, unhealthy, …
9. "feared"	suggests intensity of loathing
10. "controlled/ eliminated"	such was their disgust that containment/total destruction were the only solutions
11. use in general of words to do with illness and disease: "cholera-ridden", "tumour", "polluted", "squalor"	to them London was synonymous with infection, death, despair, …

Sentence structure:

12. balance of opening sentence ("Having invented . . . Britain promptly reeled back")	emphasises their instantaneous rejection of their own creation
13. accumulation of disturbing adjectives in second sentence ("cholera-ridden", "hideous", "polluted")	emphasises the Victorians' all-consuming, pervasive sense of horror
14. list at the end of the second sentence ("squalor, disease and crime")	emphasises the scale and diversity of the problems which disturbed them
15. positioning of "In their eyes" at beginning of final sentence	underlines how personal and immediate this problem was
16. list at end of final sentence ("feared, controlled and, if possible, eliminated")	brings the paragraph to a climax in which he sums up their revulsion through their desire to take action against their creation
17. insertion of "if possible"	creates a dramatic pause before the menacing punchline of "eliminated" and/or suggests a sense of desperation/determination
18. the relative punchiness of the final sentence (after the rather labyrinthine nature of the second sentence)	drives home the absolute negativity/certainty of their attitude

4. *Marks will depend on the quality of comment on appropriate language feature(s).*
   A single insightful comment will be worth up to 2 marks; more basic comments will be worth up to 1 mark each.
   Possible answers are:

1. "finally"	suggests this moment was one the world had been waiting for impatiently
2. "swallowed the world"	(use of personification) presents "the city" as some kind of all-conquering monster: brutal, ravenous, insatiable, greedy, unstoppable, …
3. "swallowed"	suggests an all-engulfing consumption; the change is abrupt, final and irreversible
4. "the world"	hyperbole stresses the huge scale of the change
5. "overtook"	suggests a race in which those in the city are moving forward at pace, leaving their rivals trailing behind

6. "left behind"	(continuation of "race" imagery) suggests people in the country are not making progress, inferior
7. "in the fields"	associates people living in the country with a very basic, almost primitive way of life
8. "fundamental"	stresses essential, primary nature of the change
9. "species change"	suggests an evolutionary shift
10. "like … agriculture"	use of comparison to another fundamental moment in man's evolution to stress great importance

5. *There must be some attempt to use own words.*
   Marks will depend on the quality of explanation. A clear explanation will be worth 2 marks; a more basic explanation will be worth 1 mark.
   Possible answer for 2 marks is:
   The city is "mankind's greatest invention" because it encompasses all aspects of life from fundamental issues (such as utilities, finance, transportation, law and order) to less vital issues (such as leisure facilities).

6. *There must be some attempt to use own words.*
   Any two of the following for 1 mark each:
   1. they help people/incomers to improve themselves ("engine of growth", "sustaining generation after generation of newcomers")
   2. they help (poor) people to become financially better off ("prosperity")
   3. they help to liberate people ("freedom")
   4. (as exemplified by London) they have a cohesive, individual strength ("a far stronger sense of … its identity")
   5. (as exemplified by London) they develop in a natural, progressive, methodical, organised way ("layer on layer", "sustaining generation after generation of newcomers")

7. (a) *There must be some attempt to use own words.*
   Marks will depend on the quality of the explanation. A clear explanation will be worth 2 marks; a more basic explanation will be worth 1 mark.
   Possible answers are:

1. "chapel… synagogue… mosque"	religious diversity: over time, one building has been used as a centre of worship for three major religions (Christianity, Judaism, Islam)
2. "residential (core)… banking (centre)" **and/or** "sheltering in…world's biggest"	living/housing area became business/financial area from protected, insular, inward-looking to globally pre-eminent

3. "market halls and power stations…art galleries and piazzas"	shift from the functional (suppliers of food and energy) to catering for a more cultural, aesthetic, sophisticated, leisure-related lifestyle
4. "clerks of the Great Western Railway… largest Sikh community outside India"	shift in culture, religion, ethnicity

(b) *Marks will depend on the quality of comment. A single insightful comment will be worth 2 marks; more basic comments will be worth up to 1 mark each.*
For full marks, candidates should focus on:

1. parallel openings ("Its old residential core", "Its market halls and power stations", "Its simple terraced streets")	any/all of these features are used to stress the repetitive nature, widespread scale and perhaps the inevitability of change
2. repeated "before and after" formula	
3. similar verb pattern "has made the transition", "have become" (twice)	

Comments on other features of sentence structure could be rewarded if there is some attempt to link them to the paragraph "as a whole".

8. *Marks will depend on the quality of comment on the image. An insightful comment could score up to 2 marks; a more basic comment will be worth up to 1 mark.*
Answers must show recognition of the literal root of the image and then explore how the writer is extending it figuratively.
Possible answer:
an "à la carte menu" allows diners to make an individual choice from a varied, extensive list of dishes; by using it here, the writer is suggesting that people in London are able to make a series of individual lifestyle choices from a very wide variety of activities, jobs, cultures, pursuits.
N.B. A candidate who focuses exclusively on ideas of sophistication, class or quality implied by the image may also score up to 2 marks.

9. (a) *There must be some attempt to use own words.*
Possible answers are:
1. successful cities take a flexible approach, whereas unsuccessful cities are inflexible
2. successful cities are open to change and innovation, whereas unsuccessful cities are set in their ways
3. successful cities offer a lot of choice, whereas unsuccessful cities offer little or no choice
4. successful cities are receptive to the needs of their people, whereas unsuccessful cities treat their citizens in a domineering way
5. successful cities encourage the unexpected, whereas unsuccessful cities are unadventurous/predictable
An answer need not state both sides of the issue. A clear articulation of one element will inevitably imply an understanding of the other.
N.B. Answers which become so bogged down in detail and exemplification – so that the fundamental difference is hard to discern – are unlikely to gain the mark.

(b) *Marks will depend on the quality of comment on appropriate language feature(s). A single insightful comment will be worth up to 2 marks; more basic comments will be worth up to 1 mark each.*
There will be a variety of acceptable approaches to this question. Some candidates may choose to make fairly broad comments covering the sweep of the three paragraphs; others may choose to exemplify a chosen feature by much tighter analysis of a smaller part of the text.
Possible answers are:
Contrast/Balance/Juxtaposition:

1. frequent switches between aspects of successful and unsuccessful cities throughout the three paragraphs	rapidfire approach allows strengths to be set against weaknesses time and time again to persuasive effect
2. "options open", "possibility of change" as opposed to "stuck", "rigid", "no way out"	flexibility versus rigidity
3. "allow people to be …" as opposed to "force them to be …"	(parallel construction highlights) freedom of choice versus coercion
4. "room for more than the obvious", "open to new ideas" as opposed to "closed its mind to the future"	innovation versus rigid adherence to the status quo

Repetition:

5. repetition of words to do with flexibility, opportunity, innovation etc	drives home relentlessly the positive aspect of the writer's argument
6. repetition of words to do with rigidity, lack of opportunity, coercion etc	drives home forcefully the negative aspect of the writer's argument
7. brutally repetitive openings to the sentences – "The cities that work", "The cities that are stuck", "A successful city is", "A city that has been trapped" etc	stress the writer's belief that there is a stark contrast between the two
8. repetitive "successful city"/"unsuccessful city" formula (often involving the use of parallel construction)	renders unequivocal the positive/negative distinctions the writer is making
9. repetition in general of various contrasts between successful and unsuccessful cities	hammers home his points, bludgeons the reader into submission

Climax:

10. possible climax in the final paragraph: the detailed, varied portrait of what "a successful city" has to offer is captured in a complex sentence; this is followed by the short, abrupt, definitive dismissal of "an unsuccessful city"

Word choice:

11. For full marks on word choice alone the difference must be demonstrated by referring to and commenting appropriately on at least one example from each of the lists given below.

For "a successful city", answers should make acceptable comment on the positive connotations of any of the following:

"options open … possibility of change … open to new ideas … room for surprises … room for more than the obvious … the unexpected … generating the spark … a life shared with strangers"

For "an unsuccessful city", answers should make acceptable comment on the negative connotations of any of the following:

"stuck … overwhelmed … rigid … state-owned … no way out … slums … poverty … trapped … traps …gentrification … trouble generating the spark … force(s) … ban … closed its mind"

Questions on Passage 2

10. (a) *There must be some attempt to use own words.*
Any one of the following for 1 mark:
1. important for industry/manufacture
2. second only to London as Imperial symbol
3. important for international commerce

(b) *There must be some attempt to use own words.*
Any one of the following for 1 mark:
1. important contribution to the arts/heritage/vibrant lifestyle
2. important as a shopping/commercial centre
3. continues to be "role model"/have impact, sway on other cities

(c) *Marks will depend on the quality of comment on appropriate language feature(s). A single insightful comment will be worth up to 2 marks; more basic comments will be worth up to 1 mark each.*

Possible answers are:

Word choice:

1. "pull"	suggests strong attraction
2. "buzz"	gives a sense of business and activity
3. "excitement"	suggests a sense of stimulation
4. "style"	suggests elegance, class
5. "sense of… own importance"	suggests self confidence, awareness of status in the world
6. "potent"	suggests powerful, important and far-reaching
7. "reach"	suggests the extent of Glasgow's effect
8. "influence"	suggests extent to which it is used by other cities as model, trend-setter
9. "global"	suggests influence is worldwide, far-reaching, beyond the parochial

Imagery:

10. "reach"	the sphere of Glasgow's influence is like a human arm stretching to affect things far away
11. "weaves … threads … tapestry"	extended image from the making of decorative cloth suggesting the complex connections between Glasgow and other parts/aspects of the Empire (N.B. individual words in the extended image could be dealt with as discrete images)

Sentence structure:

12. list beginning "pull, buzz … (and … and … own importance)"	has the effect of showing a number of vibrant ideas associated with Glasgow, (added to again and again by the repetition of "and" and reaching a climax in the words "own importance")
13. colon plus explanation	"global urban tapestry" is expanded to illustrate the geographical extent and the sheer number of cities influenced by Glasgow
14. list of names after dash	illustrating the variety and far-flung nature of Glasgow's renown
15. single short declarative sentence beginning with "And"	gives a final unexpected and extreme example clinching the notion of Glasgow's fame

11. (a) Gloss on "radical" for 1 mark – eg original, drastic, far-reaching, fundamentally different, …
Gloss on "derivative" for 1 mark – eg unoriginal, imitative, copied, …

(b) *Marks will depend on the quality of comment on appropriate language feature(s).*

Possible answers:

Word choice:

11. (b) continued

1. "constant"	suggests an exaggerated insistence on the success
2. "proclamation"	suggests a deliberately insistent declaration – possibly unjustified
3. "felt"	suggests the illusory nature of the innovations
4. "derivative"	suggests that Glasgow is second best – a mere copy of other earlier city developments
5. "diminishing returns"	suggests that routinely the advantages of the makeover have been becoming relentlessly smaller as time passes
6. "celebrity"	suggests taking advantage of passing or fleeting popularity rather than tried and tested expertise
7. "(reduced to a) formula"	suggests that the developments are merely copying other cities' attempts with no vestige of originality

Imagery:

8. "wind coming out of the sails"	just as a sailing vessel's progress is halted by its losing the wind which propels it, so Glasgow's supposed progress as a new and changed city is coming to a halt
9. "makeover path"	just as the instant changes wrought on people and houses are often striking but not lasting or of any real worth, the attempts to change the city have been too artificial and possibly too speedy to be really satisfying/the end of a natural or organic process

Sentence structure:

10. list after the colon	provides an extension of the artificial inflation of the alleged advantages (as above in points 1 and 2)
11. repetition of "will"	highlights/derides the over-insistence/over-confidence of the Establishment's stance
12. "But ..."	signals a move in the direction of overt criticism of the city's attempts
13. sentences beginning "What felt ..." and "When every ..."	delay the principal idea to the end of the sentence(s) for greater impact on negative ideas such as "diminishing returns" or "reduced to a formula"

12. (a) *There must be some attempt to use own words. The following points for 1 mark each*:
1. gloss on the idea of "deep inequalities ... sharp divisions" (in the socio-economic sphere) – eg extensive unfairness, discrimination, separation, ...
2. gloss on "unsustainable" in the financial sphere – eg the impossibility of continuing on the present financial course, ...
3. the idea of the deadening monotony and sameness of tourist cities

(b) *Marks will depend on the quality of comment. A single insightful comment will be worth up to 2 marks; a more basic point will be worth 1 mark.*

Possible points and comments are:

1. simple declarative sentence "There are several ..."	sets up clearly and plainly the expectation of a number of examples of the problems in the remainder of the paragraph
2. "One ... Another ... And yet another"	to signal each of the three problems separately allowing each to be readily identified
3. cumulative effect of "One ... Another ... And yet another"	culminates in the "problem" which has been the subject of the article up to this point in the passage
4. increasing length and detail devoted to each problem	highlights the most important problem (so far)
5. parenthesis/list (lines 25-26)	allows writer to demonstrate/mock the type of tedious, predictable, formulaic campaign of which he is so dismissive

13. (a) *There must be some attempt to use own words. Any of the following for 1 mark*:
1. their hypocrisy
2. their methods are paternalistic/"nanny knows best"
3. the solutions are imposed from on high/any consultation is sham
4. they have low expectations of what can be achieved

(b) *Marks will depend on the quality of comment on appropriate language feature(s). A single insightful comment will be worth up to 2 marks; more basic comments will be worth up to 1 mark each.*
Answers may not necessarily make explicit reference to tone, but there should be some recognition of the pejorative nature of the writer's use of language.

Word choice:

1. "talk the language"	suggests that there is something artificial or pretended about what these people say – they are using "jargon" rather than sincere language
2. "(do not) really (believe)"	suggests that in their heart of hearts they do not mean what they actually say
3. "impose"	suggests an opposition to "choice" etc rather than the flexibility which their "language" suggests
4. "set menu"	suggests a lack of choice, contrary to their declared intentions
5. "confident (that they know best)"	suggests an overweening adult superiority over those who they have said should be allowed to make choices
6. "rhetoric"	suggests overblown, artificial and exaggerated language intended to persuade or browbeat

Word choice (continued):

7. "old-fashioned"	suggests they are out of touch with the ideals of modern democracy
8. "top-down (approach)"	suggests that they are "on top" in matters of decision making and such things should not be left to those lower down in the heap
9. "institutional"	suggests the rigid, authoritarian, hide-bound views which permeate an organisation despite individual attempts to change it
10. "experts and professionals"	suggests that ordinary citizens are too ignorant to know what is best because they are not professionally qualified

Imagery:

11. "set menu … à la carte"	the reference to the choice or lack of choice offered in a restaurant illustrates the writer's disapproval of the establishment not offering any choice to the people of Glasgow despite their statements that there is to be "choice"

Punctuation:

12. the use of inverted commas round "opportunity", "choice" or "diversity"	shows that the writer does not believe that these concepts are on offer, or are really meant and that he disapproves of the people who are misleading the public

14. *There must be some attempt to use own words.*
Any of the following for 1 or 2 marks depending on the quality of understanding demonstrated:
1. gloss on "this unity…be mobilized in a more sustained way"
2. gloss on "bridge the gap between the city and its people" eg diminish the gulf between the governed and the governors/the people and the establishment
3. people should be allowed more say/more choice in the way the city is run/not have one model imposed on them

Question on both Passages

15. Note that the question is on "ideas", not language or style. While some candidates might make judicious use of some reference to stylistic matters to support a valid point about ideas, the thrust of a successful answer must be clearly about the writers' ideas.

The mark for this question should reflect the overall quality of the response and may not be directly related to the length of the response or to the number of points/references made. A succinct, sophisticated response should be worth more than a series of fairly trivial and obvious references. "Ticking and adding up" is not appropriate (or fair) here.

For full marks there must be reference to both passages (although not necessarily a balanced treatment) and convincing evaluative comment. Where reference is made to one passage only, the maximum mark is 3.

The following guidelines should be followed:

5 marks   clear and intelligent understanding of both passages; evaluative comment is thoughtful and convincing

4 marks   clear understanding of both passages; evaluative comment is reasonably convincing

3 marks   understanding of both passages; there is some evaluative comment

2 marks   some understanding of both passages; at least one appropriate evaluative comment

1 mark   one or two relevant but unconvincing comments

0 marks   irrelevant, or too generalised; or excessive quotation/reference without comment

The following points could be referred to by way of justifying the candidate's preference:

Passage 1

Generally unbiased and optimistic for the future.

* large scale of growth in cities
* strong Victorian view that cities represented danger
* in 2008, the number of urban dwellers exceeded the number of rural dwellers greatly
* the future success of individual cities depends on how serious issues and less serious issues are dealt with
* cities must be a "positive force" – offering the less affluent country people a chance of success and more opportunity
* examples of growth and change in London
* London's success is attributed to the width of choice; in contrast a village discourages diversity
* successful cities embrace change
* unsuccessful cities adopt a more rigid, conservative approach and do not consider the future.

Passage 2

Generally biased and more critical.

* Glasgow has always undergone change
* Glasgow is exciting, vibrant and important
* Glasgow has international status
* the city's development plan claims success in business, education and tourism but in reality has adopted a formulaic approach
* "official" Glasgow promotes a reputation for "conspicuous consumption" but it is still a city of "deep inequalities"
* establishment claims of offering "opportunity", "choice" and "diversity" are unconvincing
* establishment claims lack of success due to the poor attitudes of the people
* division between the "powerful" and the "powerless" is the nub of the problem
* unity between the city and the people is the way ahead.

ENGLISH HIGHER
CRITICAL ESSAY 2010

Please see the Critical Essay guidelines for the English Higher 2012 on page 117.

ENGLISH HIGHER
CLOSE READING 2011

1. (a) *Marks will depend on the quality of comment. An insightful comment on one word could score up to 2 marks; more basic comments will be worth up to 1 mark each. Reference alone: 0. Possible answers are:*

1. "enriches"	suggests that reading adds to one's knowledge, awareness; is rewarding, beneficial; improves one
2 "the mind"	suggests reading is influencing something greater than just the brain; it influences our consciousness: thought, perception, emotions and imagination
3 "deadens"	suggests video games make kids less aware, less sensitive, less vigorous; they make kids think less; lifeless
4 "zoning out"	suggests video games make kids detached from people and things around them, unresponsive, unstimulated

(b) *There must be some attempt to use own words.*
Clear explanation: 2 marks; less assured explanation: 1 mark.
A full gloss of "intellectual virtues in their own right" will be sufficient for 2 marks, although many candidates will acceptably gloss "different from, but comparable to, reading" in dealing with the "in their own right" part.
Possible answer:
The writer is asking if these other forms of culture:
- involve discrete thinking skills/have qualities which benefit, stimulate, challenge, stretch our minds in ways which are different from – but just as important as – reading

(c) *Marks will depend on the quality of comment. Insightful comment on one feature could score up to 3 marks; alternatively a candidate could make more basic comments for up to 1 mark each. For full marks, there must be comment on at least two features.*
For full marks, there must be coverage of both the writer's positive view and the critics' negative view.
Possible answers are:
Imagery:
When dealing with imagery, answers must show recognition of the literal root of the image and then explore how the writer is extending it figuratively.

1. "(progressive) story"	"story" suggests a developing, organised narrative: the writer sees the positive influence of popular culture as gradual, logical, coherent, interesting…
	"story" might also be linked to the idea of a news story: just as a news story is something important, topical, developing which people should know about, the writer sees the positive influence of popular culture as something of ongoing importance which he wants to make people aware of.

2 "our brains sharper"	just as sharpening involves giving cutting tools a better edge, this suggests making our brains keener, more accurate...
3 "we soak in"	soaking in is a process of absorption, of taking in as much liquid as possible; this suggests we become immersed in popular culture, that its influence is natural, irresistible, all-consuming, profound, deep...
4 "(lowbrow) fluff"	fluff is light, downy material (for example, small pieces of wool); its use suggests critics believe popular culture is light, trivial, worthless, superficial, irrelevant, trifling....
5 "honing"	just as honing is a process of giving cutting tools a perfect edge, this suggests gradually making our brains as sharp as possible, more and more precise, accurate, productive...

Some candidates may choose to deal with "sharper" and "honing" as a pair. This will be a reasonable approach. Some candidates will choose to deal with words listed under "Imagery" as word choice.

Word choice:

6. "allege"	casts doubt on, calls the critics' views into question
7 "dumbing down"	suggests popular culture offers people a reduced intellectual challenge **or** is responsible for making people less educated, less intelligent, more lowbrow
8 "progressive"	developing, advancing, moving forward steadily, leading to improvement
9 "story"	something that is developing and interesting; something that people should know about
10 "steadily"	reliable, consistent progress
11 "imperceptibly"	change is gradual, subtle
12 "sharper"	keener, more precise, more accurate
13 "soak in"	not a superficial process; influence is deep; we are fully engaged, absorbed
14 "dismissed"	brushed aside, considered beneath contempt, irrelevant, unimportant, trivial
15 "so much"	dismissive expression, heightening the sense of inconsequentiality
16 "lowbrow"	vulgar, anti-intellectual, uncultured, plebeian
17 "fluff"	worthless, trivial, inconsequential, superficial
18 "increasingly"	popular culture is more and more important
19 "honing"	sharpening, perfecting, refining
20 "skills"	desirable talents

21 some candidates may comment on the writer's repetitive use of adverbial 'developing' words which add weight to the idea of "progressive story": "steadily", "imperceptibly", "increasingly"

Sentence structure:

22 balanced structure/ contrast of "Where...story"	allows the writer to trump the critics' argument. This is heightened by the greater certainty of his "see" set against the dubious nature of their "allege"
23 use of colon	to introduce a full development of his "progressive story" argument
24 use of parenthesis "but... imperceptibly"	to explain that this positive development is so gradual that it's easy for the less astute (like the critics) to miss it
25 positioning of "I hope to persuade you" at the start of the final sentence	alerts the reader to the fact that the writer is about to make what he believes is his most important point
26 positioning of "increasingly" just before his key statement	stresses that the point he is about to make is more and more relevant, true
27 balanced nature of final statement, hinging on the "just as important as" comparison	stresses skills developed by popular culture are of a comparable standard to the skills developed by reading

2. (a) *sentence structure;*
   Marks will depend on the quality of comment. A single insightful comment will be worth 2 marks; more basic comments will be worth up to 1 mark each. Mere identification of a feature of sentence structure: 0.
   Possible answers are:

1 positioning of (or rhythmic/ repetitive nature of) "And the first and last thing"	definitive "alpha and omega" nature of this phrase, especially when placed at the start of the sentence, suggests the difficulty of video games is a fundamental point to the writer
2 use of parenthesis "the thing ...hear"	adds to the mystery, adds to the dramatic build-up to the final announcement of video games' difficulty
3 additional phrase "sometimes maddeningly"	two functions: again adds to the build-up and/or ramps up the notion of extreme difficulty that "fiendishly" has introduced
4 Candidates may attempt a more general point, incorporating aspects of points 1–3, about the various ways in which the writer builds up to/delays the climax of the (ultimately slightly lame) "hard"	
5 use of climax in the sentence "The dirty ...fun."	somewhat awkward/unusual construction of this sentence is designed to stress the "not having fun" element of its conclusion
6 repetition of the "you may be" structure	stresses – and this is heightened by the use of the inclusive direct address – the variety of problems playing video games may cause

7 list of adjectives ("frustrated", "confused", "disorientated", "stuck")	rat-a-tat run of adjectives suggests 'the sea of troubles' playing video games may involve
8 anticlimax(?) of "you may be stuck"	in its definitive downbeat simplicity, it is a stark summation of the seemingly insoluble challenge these games present
9 use of the continuous tense in final sentence	an argument might be made that this reflects the ongoing, nagging nature of the problems involved

(b) *imagery*

Marks will depend on the quality of comment. A single insightful comment will be worth 2 marks; more basic comments will be worth up to 1 mark each.

When dealing with imagery, answers must show recognition of the literal root of the image and then explore how the writer is extending it figuratively.

Possible answers are:

1 "stuck"	to be stuck is to be fixed immovably; it suggests being trapped in a situation which offers no escape
2 "wrestling"	wrestling involves close, physical combat with a single opponent; it suggests a demanding, exhausting battle with an unforgiving enemy
3 "worrying a loose tooth"	involves the constant working away at a persistent physical annoyance; it suggests that the difficulties presented by video games are nagging frustrations that constantly prey on one's mind

NB Comment could possibly be made on "dirty little secret", but it will be hard to relate this convincingly to "the difficulties of playing video games". It could be argued that the expression is usually used in the realms of ethics or morality, a deliberate attempt to hide the truth, a cover-up of some sort, a hidden scandal; used in relation to the difficulty of video games, it heightens the potentially damaging nature of this feature, suggests it is a very negative feature that is deliberately glossed over.

3. (a) *There must be some indication that the candidate understands the term "irony". A "two-pronged" answer is required.*
Possible answer:
   - young people are very averse to doing mundane, repetitive tasks but will happily play video games which involve more drudgery than fun, are full of mundane, repetitive tasks

(b) *There must be some attempt to use own words.*
For full marks, candidates need to show an understanding of the distinction between "delayed gratification" (video games) and "instant gratifications" (most forms of popular entertainment). If a full gloss of one term suggests a clear understanding of its converse, full marks should be awarded.
Possible answer:
   - most forms of popular entertainment offer quick, immediate, easily gained pleasure, reward, satisfaction but the pleasure, reward, satisfaction from video games

is very slow in coming, takes a long time to achieve, seems as though it will never come

4. (a) *There must be some attempt to use own words.*
Candidates must focus on why the "rewards" benefit "the learning process". Merely describing the "rewards" fails to address the question properly.
For full marks, answers must cover the key idea in point 1 below plus any of points 2-9. A good explanation of point 1 will be worth 2 marks.
   1. people are hard-wired to respond strongly to rewards; people's brains are created in such a way that they find rewards a great stimulus to action, learning etc
   2. video games are designed to be full of rewards
   3. rewards in video games are precise, with clear outcomes (gloss of "clearly defined")
   4. the rewards are attractive
   5. the rewards are presented in a variety of forms
   6. players are constantly reminded about the rewards
   7. the rewards are vitally important to achieving success in the games
   8. the rewards are more intense, striking, colourful than in real life
   9. players aren't always aware that they are learning (gloss on "without realising ...")

(b) *Marks will depend on the quality of comment. A single insightful comment will be worth 2 marks; more basic comments will be worth up to 1 mark each.*
Possible answers are:
Word choice:

1 "everywhere"	suggests rewards are all around, presenting an infinite set of possible attractions
2 "(gaming) universe"	a vast, multi-faceted environment of infinite possibilities
3 "teeming"	suggests a vibrant superabundance; brimful of lively attractions
4 "deliver"	suggests video games are productive, make good their promises, fulfil expectations
5 "spells"	something magical, enchanting, wondrous
6 "vivid"	colourful, intense, attractive, striking

Sentence structure:

7 use of list ("more life ...new spells.")	suggests variety, large number of rewards
8 brevity of each example in the list ("more life ... new spells.")	heightens the "teeming" idea: no time for a detailed description, there are so many aspects they come tumbling out at a rapid, almost breathless rate
9 repetition of "new"	stresses the fresh challenges that abound, never-ending novelties on offer
10 (repeated) use of comparatives in final sentence	stresses idea that video games are superior to life itself in a variety of ways
11 repetitive, rhythmic build-up in final sentence ("and more ... and more")	heightens the sense of the writer having an ever-expanding range of positive points to make about rewards in video games

5. (a) *There must be some attempt to use own words.*
   Any two of the following for 1 mark each:
   1 the games may seem attractive but the attractions flatter to deceive, are rather superficial, blind one to the truth ("dazzled")
   2 subject matter of the games is infantile, petty, puerile, trivial... ("actual content ... childish")
   3 unnecessarily threatening, unjustifiably scary ("gratuitously menacing" – but gloss on "menacing" alone: 0)
   4 the subject matter is very limited **and/or** moves between the two extremes of violence and childish fantasy ("alternates ... princess-rescuing")
   5 violent ("drive-by shooting")
   6 pure fantasy ("princess-rescuing")

   (b) *Marks will depend on the quality of comment. A single insightful comment will be worth 2 marks; more basic comments will be worth up to 1 mark each.*
   Possible answers are:

1 (repeated) use of "just" in opening sentence (plus the "perhaps")	the effect of these words is to diminish, downplay, minimise the importance of what might appear to be absolute fundamentals: winning the game, completing the story or being wowed by the graphics
2 structure of the first sentence	sense of lumping together three apparently vital elements of the game so they can be somewhat undermined *en bloc*
3 "dazzled"	suggests one's vision being impaired, being over-impressed by superficial details, being blinded to the truth
4 "draws you in"	suggests a rather devious, deceptive process
5 capitalisation of "Next Thing"	could suggest something rather childishly overblown about people's curiosity, mockery of exaggerated importance
6 "childish"	suggests simple, undemanding, infantile, puerile
7 "gratuitously"	suggests pointless, unnecessary, unjustifiable
8 "drive-by shooting and princess-rescuing"	deliberately polarised, reductive, black and white view of the content of video games
9 "drive-by shooting"	particularly cowardly, unpleasant, unheroic, random form of violence
10 "princess-rescuing"	very simplistic, fantastical, childish, fairy tale-esque
11 (balanced) structure of final sentence	importance of actual content rejected with brisk, unarguable certainty, followed by developed endorsement of the reward system (this contrast heightened by the "It is not...it is" balance around semi-colon)

6. *There must be some attempt to use own words.*
   Clear explanation: 2 marks; less assured explanation: 1 mark.
   Possible answer (Algebra):
   • many people see algebra as pointless, abstract, irrelevant, but studying it develops their brain power, adds rigour to the way they think

Possible answer (Chess):
• many people see chess as a game which has a straightforward objective or is abstract or is about (glorifying) war and battles, or presenting war and battles in a formulaic way, but playing it develops strategic, tactical thinking, adds rigour to the way they think

7. (a) *Marks will depend on the quality of comment. For full marks, there must be recognition of the contrast.*
   Possible answers are:

1 (repeated) use of the conditional "may"	suggests some uncertainty about the impact of novels **or** that the efficacy of novels is somewhat haphazard (especially when set against the definite, irresistible "force" of video games)
2 "activate (our imagination)"	suggests setting something in motion, a more gradual process perhaps (than the more immediate and more strategic thinking skills video games demand)
3 "conjure up"	suggests a somewhat magical, mystical, dreamy, ethereal process
4 parallel construction in "Novels ...emotions"	suggests something very measured, unhurried, perhaps even languid, about the outcomes of reading novels
5 "force"	video games are much more compelling, active, immediate, dynamic (especially when set against the uncertain "may" of novels)
6 switch from "our" to "you"	suggests playing video games is a more direct, personal activity
7 list of verbs ("to analyse ... to decide")	rapid fire, punchy run of infinitives suggests playing video games is a very dynamic, frenetic activity which involves a lot of cerebral processes taking place simultaneously
8 nature of verbs in the list	all the verbs are to do with higher order thinking skills and so stress the cerebral nature of playing video games
9 some candidates will highlight the very different structures of the two "halves" of the sentence, picking up on some of the ideas from points 1, 4 and 7; this may well be a profitable approach to take	

   (b) *Marks will depend on the quality of comment. For full marks, there must be recognition of the contrast.*
   Possible answers are:
   Gamer from "the outside":

1 "looks like"	suggests this may be an unreliable perspective, a superficial, unquestioning way to approach an analysis of gamers
2 "fury"	suggests the gamer is behaving in an impulsive, uncontrolled way; everything is being done at top speed, in a blur of unthinking activity
3 "clicking"	suggests mindless, repetitive activity
4 "shooting"	suggests destructive, homicidal activity
5 "clicking and shooting"	automatic, unthinking, mechanical, robotic, repetitive…

6 it could be argued that the general simplicity of the penultimate sentence (especially when compared to the much more complex final sentence) heightens the impression that this is a naïve, simplistic way to view gamers

"inside the gamer's mind"

7 "if you"	deliberate attempt to involve the reader in what is presented as the much more pro-active, cerebral, sophisticated, subtle approach to analysing gamers
8 "peer"	suggests an active approach involving close examination
9 "mind"	suggests thinking, rational being
10 re-introduction of "the primary activity"	heightens impression that the ideas in this sentence supersede the wrong-headed thinking of the previous sentence
11 "turns out"	sense of some kind of revelation, surprise, discovery
12 "another creature"	suggests something mysterious, surprising, unexpected, interesting but hard to define, a new form of life we didn't know existed
13 "altogether"	heightens the idea of a complete turnaround, of the complete reversal of received wisdom
14 use of colon	to introduce detailed description of the full range of intellectual activities involved in gaming
15 balance/ repetition of "some of them"	stresses range of activities involved
16 contrast "snap judgements … long-term strategies"	again shows range of important decision-making skills involved from quick, smart thinking to overall planning
17 "decisions"/ "judgements"	suggests wise, fair thinking
18 "strategies"	suggests considered, creative thinking

19 it could be argued that the variety, complexity and punchiness of this sentence (especially when compared to the much simpler preceding sentence) heightens the impression that it contains a much more persuasive, well-rounded argument

Relevant to both "inside" and "outside"

20 "But …"	positioning at the start of the sentence flags up a significant transition between the two viewpoints

8. (a) *There must be some attempt to use own words.*
Any two of the following for 1 mark each:

1 the unreasonable, hysterical behaviour ("snarl", "sobbing", "shrieking", "pleading")
2 games are played compulsively, obsessively; young people cannot live without them ("narcotic withdrawal", "addicts", "hooked")
3 disastrous consequences for the ability to read ("catastrophic effect . . . on the literacy")
4 disastrous consequences for young boys' future chances of success ("catastrophic effect . . . on the prospects of young males")

(b) *Marks will depend on the quality of comment. For full marks there must be some recognition of the hyperbolic/exaggerated nature of the writing. A single insightful comment will be worth 2 marks; more basic comments will be worth up to 1 mark each.*

Possible answers are:

1 an overall recognition (supported by some suitable exemplification) of how the hyperbolic nature of the writing is used to create a rather artificial outrage should score 2 marks

The following specific points could be commented on relevantly:

2 "snarl … sobbing and shrieking and horrible pleading … wail of protest"	over-dramatising of children's reactions, suggesting extreme, sometimes animalistic behaviour
3 "narcotic withdrawal … drug … addicts"	exaggerating the connection between gaming and serious illness, dependency
4 "strobing colours"	suggests extreme disorientating effect
5 "Millions"	exaggeratedly vast scale of the problem
6 "hooked"	as point 3 above
7 "it is time someone had the guts to stand up, cross the room, and just say no to Nintendo"	definitive statement of intent to carry out decisive action to stop gaming activity
8 "just say no to Nintendo"	tongue-in-cheek allusion to "just say no" campaign tagline; also first in sequence of exaggerated alliteration
9 repetition of "it is time" and "it is about time"	stresses writer's sense of exasperation
10 "garrotte the Game Boy"/ "paralyse the PlayStation"	hyperbolic acts of destruction (highlighted by alliteration)
11 sequence of alliterative, game-related phrases	intensifies the sense of increasing anger; self-conscious over-use of stylistic feature

12 "as a society, that we admitted"	sense of full-scale communal guilt for which we must accept responsibility
13 "the catastrophic effect"	overly dramatic description of the disastrous consequences
14 "these blasted gizmos"	use of slang to show his utter contempt for pointless gadgets

9. *For full marks both school and home must be dealt with in order to explore the contrast.*
Marks will depend on the quality of comment.
Possible answers are:
School:

1 "demand"	suggests sense of authoritative claim
2 "provide"	suggests nurturing, caring
3 "expect"	suggests responsibility for child's learning lies with the school
4 "fill"	suggests idea of achieving capacity
5 "love (of books)"	suggests intensity of emotion, goes beyond the merely functional

Home:

6 "slump"	suggests unthinking passivity, slovenly posture and attitude
7 "hedonistic"	suggests selfish pursuit of (parents') own pleasures
8 "some other (room)"	vagueness suggests lack of concern, couldn't-care-less attitude
9 "nippers"	suggests a rather demeaning, patronising, offhand attitude
10 "bleeping and zapping"	suggests pointless, repetitive, noisy, slightly aggressive
11 "speechless rapture"	suggests hypnotic state where words are superfluous
12 "passive"	suggests no active responsibility taken for their learning/ no real engagement on the children's part
13 "washed"	suggests completely covered, submerged, not under control
14 "explosions and gore"	suggests excess of mindless violence
15 "so long"	suggests prolonged inactivity which seems to lead to their being absorbed by the machine
16 "sucked"	suggests surrender of their very being

10. *Marks will depend on the quality of comment. A strong comment could score up to 2 marks; more basic comments will score up to 1 mark each.*
Possible answers are:

1 "blinking lizards"	far from enhancing education, the effect is to turn children into a lower form of life
2 "motionless"	suggests children are inactive, semi-conscious, death-like, ...
3 "twitching"	suggests only barely alive, making vague spasm-like movements
4 "These machines"	rather sneering tone

5 "These machines teach them nothing"	short, definitive statement indicating total lack of worth
6 "no ratiocination, discovery or feat of memory"	list of worthy qualities negated by "no" to emphasise mindlessness of the games
7 "though some of them may cunningly pretend to be educational"	concessionary clause which condemns the artful falsehoods promulgated
8 "may cunningly pretend"	suggests deviousness on part of manufacturers, a despicable attempt to deceive the public
9 "looked"	suggests a deceptive outward appearance
10 "fairly historical"	disparaging use of adverb to indicate half-hearted approval of history content
11 "on the packet"	coming after comma, sounds like a pointed afterthought, as if to imply actual contents were something different
12 "guilt-ridden (parent)"	suggests sense of being burdened by pangs of conscience which are abused by unscrupulous manufacturers
13 "Phooey!"	structure: single word exclamation completely refuting the manufacturer's claims tone: utter dismissiveness through use of outlandish, mock-childish word
14 "robotically"	suggests mindless, automatic, the antithesis of learning
15 "slaughtered"	to emphasise the brutality, carnage, bloodbath
16 "and then they did it again, that was it."	monosyllabic description to suggest dull, unengaging nature of the game
17 "that was it"	tone of disbelief at meagreness of content
18 "Everything"	to emphasise the absolute paucity of content
19 "programmed"	suggests that, computer-like, there is no possibility of exercising individual choice
20 "spoon-fed"	image of helpless baby being fed, no need for the individual to think or act
21 "immediate"	to emphasise the absence of opportunity to reflect or to learn the value of effort
22 "Everything was programmed, spoon-fed, immediate"	list-like accumulation of adjectives stressing the unthinking nature of the activity
23 "endlessly showering"	suggests continuous, lavish, overwhelming, undeserved commendations
24 "bogus"	blunt condemnation of its falseness, suggesting something almost criminal
25 "massacres"	a reminder of the unsavoury content of the game

11. *There must be some attempt to use own words.*
    Acceptable gloss on
    1 "read enough to absorb the basic elements of vocabulary, grammar, rhythm, style and structure" , eg read widely in order to acquire the essential components of language (1 mark)
       and
    2 "to articulate your own thoughts in your own words" eg to express adequately your own ideas (1 mark)

12. *Marks will depend on the quality of evaluative comment. For full marks there must be attention to the idea of "conclusion" and to the "condemnation ... in the passage as a whole".*
    The following points could be made, but all points which candidates propose will be judged on their merits.

1 "So I say now:"	Churchillian call to arms which signals the start of the peroration
2 "sitting in auto-lobotomy"	recalls description used in paragraph 3 (lines 11-16), and this reminds us of the detrimental effects of video gaming on young people
3 use of imperatives - "Summon", "Steel", "yank out", "get out", "strike"	takes the reader back to the turning off of the equipment at the beginning of the passage because the writer feels action must be taken
4 "all your strength, all your courage"	rhetorical patterning to reinforce the effort required by adults to overcome their offspring's addiction
5 "sledgehammer"	cartoon-like exaggeration typical of whole passage
6 final five words "strike a blow for literacy"	brings together writer's literal and metaphorical use of the expression in the title and at the end to illustrate the value he attaches to literacy
7 tone remains consistent	faux-outrage throughout, building to this ludicrous ending
8 argues that the situation is so serious that parents need to take decisive action to remedy the problem	
9 returns to the initial scenario to remind the reader of the "logical" need to take action	

13. *Note that the question is on "ideas". A case may be made for either passage. Answers which demonstrate a clear line of argument and refer closely to the ideas of both passages to illustrate the line of thought should be rewarded.*
    The mark for this question should reflect the overall quality of the response and may not be directly related to the length of the response or to the number of points/references made. A succinct, sophisticated response should be worth more than a series of fairly trivial points and obvious references. "Ticking and adding up" is not appropriate (or fair) here.
    *For full marks there must be reference to the ideas contained in both passages (although not necessarily a balanced treatment) and convincing evaluative comment. Where reference is made to one passage only, the **maximum** mark is 3.*
    The following guidelines should be used:
    5 marks   clear and intelligent understanding of both passages; evaluative comment is thoughtful and convincing
    4 marks   clear understanding of both passages; evaluative comment is reasonably convincing
    3 marks   understanding of both passages; there is some evaluative comment
    2 marks   some understanding of both passages; at least one appropriate evaluative comment

1 mark   one or two relevant but unconvincing comments
0 marks   irrelevant, or too generalised, or excessive quotation/ reference without comment

The following points could be made, but all points which candidates propose will have to be judged on their merits:
Passage 1
- awareness of the traditional view that reading is better for the mind than video games
- writer's acknowledgement that most people will come into contact with other media
- writer's oppositional view that video games may be as mentally stimulating as reading
- the difficulties and frustrations involved in playing video games
- recognition that young people are more likely to play video games
- surprise that the onerous nature of "tasks" in video games would appeal to young people
- the popular misconception that video games offer immediate rewards
- the view that video games can promote learning in an entertaining way
- writer's belief that the reward strategy in video games is a powerful attraction
- the notion that narrative is often unimportant to the success of a video game
- the analogy of algebra/chess to illustrate the power of video games to develop critical thinking and problem-solving skills
- video games develop skills which are different from novels, music, etc
- the astonishing difference between appearance and reality in gaming activities

Passage 2
- the comparison of video games to an addictive drug
- the negative effects which video games have on children
- argument that video games are responsible for poor literacy
- argument that boys' lives may be ruined by over-exposure to video games
- hypocritical attitude of parents who expect schools to foster good literacy
- the writer's view that some video games masquerade as educational
- suggestion that the rewards in video games are undeserved
- view that reading books is essential for developing effective communication skills
- final paragraph encourages removal of video games from children

ENGLISH HIGHER CRITICAL ESSAY 2011

Please see the Critical Essay guidelines for the English Higher 2012 on page 117.

ENGLISH HIGHER
CLOSE READING 2012

[N.B. Replaced by Specimen Question Paper answers – see page 70 for details.]

Questions on Passage 1

1. (a) Acceptable gloss on "ecstatic" (1 mark) – eg joyous, thrilled, excited, delighted …; "happy" by itself is not acceptable – there must be some idea of intensity.
   Acceptable gloss on "nostalgic" (1 mark) – eg looking back fondly, wistful, regretful, reflective, … "sad/unhappy" by itself not acceptable – there must be some idea of something connected with past or the idea that he is apprehensive, fearful (at possible loss/demise of libraries) (1 mark).

   (b) Marks will depend on quality of comment on the chosen words. For full marks, two examples must be dealt with.
   Possible answers are:

1 "book-lined"	suggests large number/area of books, implying organised, impressive nature…
2 "cathedral-quiet"	connotations of solemnity, reverence, devotion, large hushed space…
3 "cherished"	suggests cared for emotionally (rather than just practically), warmth…
4 "civilisation"	connotations of that which marks us out from less sophisticated societies
5 "lose"	sense of being deprived, bereft…
6 "cultural"	suggests traditions, heritage, civilised society,…
7 "peril"	suggests threat, risk, menace, danger (to something precious)

2. Candidates could argue either way or on both sides. Marks will depend on the quality of explanation. A single basic point will be worth 1 mark; a more developed justification will be worth 2 marks. Possible answers are:
   "High priority":
   1 use of "remembered" suggests that the library, although initially overlooked, was indeed a priority
   2 despite the fact they "neglected shops and amenities", they still put in a library, which suggests that it was considered more important than these
   "Low priority":
   3 the high number (60,000) of potential users contrasted with the smallness of the facility (a "shed") suggests inadequacy
   4 use of "remembered" suggests it was an afterthought, a last-minute idea
   5 the fact it was a "wooden shed" suggests it was basic, cheap, unsophisticated, temporary and therefore considered of little importance
   6 the use of "somehow" indicates that nobody was sure why the decision had been taken; it just happened
   7 tone of "– actually, a wooden shed" as if a rather amused, sarcastic aside suggesting an afterthought, a wry admission of its inadequacies…

3. Marks will depend on the quality of comment. An insightful comment on one technique could score up to 3 marks; alternatively, a candidate could make more basic comments for up to 1 mark each. For full marks there should be comment on both imagery and word choice, but markers should be sympathetic to areas of overlap. Answers on imagery must "deconstruct" the image, ie show an understanding of the literal root of the image and then explore how the writer is extending it figuratively.
   Answers on word choice must deal with the connotative areas of the words chosen, exploring why the choice of word is effective.
   Possible answers are:
   Imagery:

1 "stretching"	gives the impression of something being pulled or elongated with connotations of never-ending, upward movement, aspiring
2 "cocooned"	as larvae are protected and self-contained in their cocoons, so each floor in the library is separate and shelters the students within their specialised knowledge areas
3 "worlds of knowledge"	the number of floors is so great and they are so separate that they are like different, independent planetary systems, each specialising in a particular area of knowledge
4 "planets"	the separation into large, distinct learning areas, each self-contained like the isolation and individualism of each planet in space

   Word choice:

5 "wonder"	connotations of awe, freshness, childlike amazement, admiration …
6 "skyscraper (library)"	slightly exaggerated description suggests size and magnificence (be sympathetic to candidates who choose to see "skyscraper" as an image)
7 "vast"	gives the impression of an enormous extent of space
8 "atrium"	idea of large, impressive central area – with connotations of classical ideas/learning
9 "devoted"	connotations of love, reverence, dedication …
10 "chatting, flirting, doodling, panicking"	(any of these) – suggestions of human foibles, ordinary behaviour contrasted with the extraordinary nature of the library
11 "exploring"	suggests excitement of new discovery, sense of quest, hint of size,…
12 "unique"	suggestions of something very special, to be marvelled at …

   N.B. words from 1-4 above could be the subject of appropriate comments as word choice.

4. (a) *Marks will depend on the quality of comment. An insightful comment on one feature could score up to 2 marks; alternatively, a candidate could make more basic comments for 1 mark each. For full marks there should be reference to more than one feature. The writer's attitude may be implicit in the candidate's answer.*
Possible answers are:
Sentence structure:

1 climactic nature of second sentence	building up from an abrupt start to the negative attitude by "chatter…at a thousand decibels" or (possibly) presenting a positive attitude in admiring their ability to communicate loudly or their ability to carry out more than one task at a time
2 use of questions	could suggest a positive attitude by backing up the idea that young people are modern and that they do not approve of subsidising libraries or combined with a mock-scornful tone could suggest that he believes the answer to the questions is that we do need libraries rather than the slick media world of the MTV generation – ie a negative attitude
3 structure of the first sentence	a case might just be made that the colon is used to introduce a demonstration of the writer's attitude that he prefers the past to the present and therefore will be critical of the MTV generation

Word choice:

4 "multi-tasking"	suggests positive attitude in that these people are seen as talented in their ability to perform several tasks simultaneously or suggests a negative attitude in that in trying to do so many things at once, due attention is not given to the important matters
5 "cheap books"	suggests positive aspects in that these books are readily available to all without recourse to a library or negatively, the books are cheap in the sense of not worth much intellectually
6 "chatter"	negative in that the word suggests inconsequential communication or positive in that it suggests easy personal interaction
7 "thousand decibels"	probably negative in that it suggests that the noise is too loud for real thought
8 "old-fashioned"	probably negative in that it suggests he thinks the MTV generation is too readily dismissive, or too keen to believe libraries are outdated

Tone:

9 derogatory	backed up by any of the comments suggested above
10 admiring	backed up by any of the comments suggested above
11 mock-scornful/ sarcastic	backed up by any of the comments suggested above

(b) A basic understanding that diminishing use of libraries leads to diminishing levels of provision, which leads to diminishing use …

5. (a) *There must be some attempt to use own words. Any four of the following for 1 mark each:*
1 idea of accessibility (ie acceptable gloss on "strategically situated")
2 idea of free access (ie acceptable gloss on "too expensive … to buy")
3 idea that resources are more sophisticated (ie acceptable gloss on "too complex to find online")
4 idea of supporting democratic responsibilities (ie acceptable gloss on "informed citizenship")
5 idea of community awareness/cohesion (ie acceptable gloss on "civic pride")
6 idea of professional support (ie acceptable gloss on "trained librarian")
7 idea of informed/refined selection (ie acceptable gloss on "honed and developed by experts")
8 idea of high standard of material (ie acceptable gloss on "quality … of information")
9 idea of authenticity (ie acceptable gloss on "veracity of information")
10 idea of selectivity of information (in contrast with junk online)

(b) *Marks will depend on the quality of comment on the words selected. For full marks the contrast must be demonstrated by referring to at least one word from each of the lists given below.*
For libraries, answers should make acceptable comment on the positive connotations of any of the following:
"trained … honed … developed … experts … guarantee … quality … veracity"
For the internet, answers should make acceptable comment on the negative connotations of any of the following:
"Achilles' heel … (of course) nonsense … cluttered … false … (plain) junk … never"

6. (a) *Any acceptable gloss, eg guardians, protectors, those who keep something safe, …*

(b) *Marks will depend on the quality of comment. An insightful comment on one example/feature could score up to 2 marks; alternatively, a candidate could make more basic comments for up to 1 mark each.*
Possible answers are:
Word choice:

1 "(become the) fashion"	connotations of transience, shallowness, …
2 "entertainment centres"/"audio-visuals"	connotations of pandering to popular taste, lack of seriousness, …
3 "gimmicks"	connotations of cheap trickery, merely to capture attention, …
4 "popularising"	connotations of dumbing down, aiming for lowest common denominator, …

5 "reduced"	connotations of loss of quality, depth, sophistication, …
6 "child's view"	connotations of naiveté, lack of sophistication, limited perspective, …

Tone:

7 grudging	"some (enthusiasm)" suggests reluctance to welcome the idea fully
8 scornful	appropriate comment based on any of 1-6 above
9 didactic	appropriate comment on lines 52-54 ("cannot always be reduced", "duty", "future generations", "invest", "culture")

Structure:

10 list ("audio-visuals, interactive displays and gimmicks") ending in the anti-climax ("gimmicks")	reduces the other items to meaningless technical tricks
11 structure of "While I have … universe"	limited concession emphasises the dismissiveness of what follows

7. Marks will depend on the quality of comment on the ideas and/or language. For full marks the concept of "the passage as a whole" must be addressed.
Possible answers are:
Ideas:
1   Google and the Bodleian Library are brought together again in this paragraph
2   The idea of large numbers (one million books) on Google/the vastness of libraries leading to an understanding of the enormous amount of material which can never be known
3   The differentiation between information and wisdom is what the passage has been leading up to

Language:

4 "Of course"	strategic concession/idea of bringing reader onside/of being reasonable – in preparation for conclusion
5 "Yet here's"	conversational tone – leading the reader to come on board and share his ideas
6 "daunting"	strong word suggesting the enormous and frightening amount of knowledge
7 "even a fraction"	suggests, in contrast, the very small proportion with which one person can come to grips
8 "Ever."	emphatic, one word sentence closing the door on the possibility of conquering all knowledge

9 "merely imbibing"	in contrast with wisdom, suggesting that information acquired simply as quantity, without understanding or context, is as mechanical as drinking
10 word order in last sentence	the inversion of normal order places the realisation very close to the "ever" which gives it more impact, and leaves the important word "wisdom" to follow its verb and take a central place in the last sentence
11 dash plus final statement in last sentence	the pause created by the dash puts emphasis on the last words ("merely imbibing information") throwing them into stronger contrast with "the beginning of wisdom" which is the thrust of the passage as a whole

Questions on Passage 2

8.   (a) *Any one of the following for 1 mark:*
1   (very) happy
2   idyllic
3   carefree
4   nostalgic
5   calm, peaceful
6   any other answer which conveys a positive feeling or the importance of the memory to the writer

    (b) *Marks will depend on the quality of comment. An insightful comment could score up to 3 marks. More basic comments will be worth up to 1 mark each.*
    Possible answers are:

1 "We are surrounded by eight million books."	the very short, declarative, unembellished sentence emphasises the simple, breathtaking fact
2 "eight million books"	overwhelming sense of quantity
3 "on every side"	awe-inspiring because books are inescapable, almost intimidating
4 "hundreds of yards deep"	the sheer scale of the collection
5 "at the rate of two miles a year"	impressive growth rate
6 "surrounded by", "Behind", "beneath"	directional details – use of a variety of prepositions and adverbial phrases of place to convey the omnipresence of books
7 "reach into the sky"	idea of towering beyond the normal, aspirational, connotations of heavenly, …
8 "(in compact) ranks"	image of armed forces which suggests the highly organised positioning of the books
9 "subterranean"	sense of dark, mysterious, alluring
10 "subterranean stacks"	alliteration suggests hushed reverence

11 "entombed in words"	image of burial suggests the all-encompassing presence of books
12 "unimaginable (volume)"	beyond the power of the mind to conceive
13 "cold storage"	sci-fi idea of some potential waiting to be revived
14 "quiet and vast and waiting"	climactic description to suggest the overpowering, slightly menacing, nature of such an enormous collection

(c) *Marks will depend on the quality of the comment. Evaluation may be implicit.*
   Possible answer:
   The repetition of "perhaps" conveys the writer's wistful uncertainty and makes the reader aware that he has a wealth of happy memories from which to choose.

9. *Marks will depend on the quality of comment on one image. An insightful comment could score up to 2 marks; a weaker comment will be worth up to 1 mark. If more than one image is discussed, mark all and award the better/best mark. Answers on imagery must "deconstruct" the image, ie show an understanding of the literal root of the image and then explore how the writer is extending it figuratively.*
   Possible comments are:

1 "temple"	just as a temple is a place of worship and reverence, a library deserves our utmost respect (because of the accumulation of knowledge which it contains)
2 "core"	just as the core is the heart, the essential part, a library is central to our lives and society
3 "citadel"	just as a citadel is a fortress, a library provides a stronghold to safeguard all that we consider most precious

10. (a) *There must be some attempt to use own words.*
   It could signal the end of conventional libraries, (which will no longer be used) (1 mark) – ie a basic understanding of "could finally destroy traditional libraries, which will become mere warehouses for the physical objects, empty of people and life" (lines 28-30).

   (b) *There must be some attempt to use own words. Any three of the following for 1 mark each:*
   1 a single catalogue will ensure that everything is stored in one place
   2 democracy – knowledge will be available to all
   3 it will be impossible to wipe out knowledge (by destroying books)
   4 totalitarian states will not be able to keep knowledge to themselves/deny it to the masses.

11. (a) *Marks will depend on the clarity of the explanation. Clear explanation: 2 marks; less assured explanation: 1 mark.*
   Either or both of the following:
   1 there is visual beauty in the book itself
   2 there is sensual pleasure in holding the actual book

(b) *Marks will depend on the clarity of the explanation. Clear explanation: 2 marks; less assured explanation: 1 mark. Any one or more of the following:*
   1 acceptable gloss on "central to our understanding of what it is to be human" – libraries allow us to find out about life and our position in it
   2 acceptable gloss on "sociable thinking, exploring and exchanging ideas" – function of libraries as a meeting place for discussion
   3 acceptable gloss on "recreational" – libraries as places of relaxation or even romance

12. *For full marks there must be reference to ideas and language, with some evaluative comment.*
   The following points could be made, but all points which candidates propose will have to be judged on their merits:
   Ideas:
   1 the film illustrates the conflict between libraries and new technology – the two main characters represent the two sides
   2 the passage ends on a positive note – libraries and online catalogue can happily co-exist

   Language/Style:
   3 literal and metaphorical marriage
   4 "smooching" – jocular, informal reference to easy, affectionate, slightly old-fashioned relationship
   5 play on words – "everyone reads happily ever after"
   6 single sentence final paragraph sums up the link between the film and the co-existence of libraries and an online catalogue

13. *The mark for this question should reflect the quality of the response in two areas:*
   • *identification of the essential areas of agreement in attitude/ideas*
   • *reference to/treatment of the ideas which inform the writers' attitudes*
   A response which clearly identifies at least three essential areas of agreement in attitude and has at least some supporting evidence will score a minimum of 3 marks.
   These essential areas of agreement are:
   1 libraries are a vital part of our culture
   2 libraries are repositories of vast amounts of learning/knowledge
   3 libraries provide access for everyone (to the physical object)
   4 libraries are part of the community/encourage sociability
   5 early experiences of libraries remain deep in the psyche
   There will inevitably be some overlap among these points (eg between 1 and 2). Markers will have to judge the extent to which a candidate has covered two points or just one.

   The following guidelines should be used:

5 marks	identification of essential areas of agreement, with an intelligent use of supporting evidence
4 marks	identification of essential areas of agreement, with sound use of supporting evidence
3 marks	identification of essential areas of agreement, with some supporting evidence
2 marks	identification of only two essential areas of agreement or identification of more than two without supporting evidence
1 mark	identification of just one essential area of agreement
0 marks	failure to identify any essential area of agreement and/or complete misunderstanding of the task

The following main ideas could be used in support, but some other points might be used successfully:

Passage 1:
- belief in the importance of "physical" libraries
- impact of early experiences (Drumchapel, Glasgow University)
- idea of libraries as part of the community
- libraries as guarantor of quality
- importance for future generations

Passage 2:
- early nostalgic memories of various libraries
- the library as the "hushed core of civilisation"
- the attraction of libraries (despite benefits of online plan)
- access to the "physical object"
- libraries as part of the community

ENGLISH HIGHER CRITICAL ESSAY 2012

1. **Judging against the Performance Criteria**

   Each essay should first be read to establish whether it achieves success in all the Performance Criteria below, including relevance and the standards for technical accuracy (see 2 below).

   Understanding

   As appropriate to task, the response demonstrates secure understanding of key elements, central concerns and significant details of the *text(s).

   Analysis

   The response explains accurately and in detail ways in which relevant aspects of structure/style/language contribute to meaning/effect/impact.

   Evaluation

   The response reveals clear engagement with the *text(s) or aspects of the text(s) and stated or implied evaluation of effectiveness, substantiated by detailed and relevant evidence from the *text(s).

   Expression

   Structure, style and language, including use of appropriate critical terminology, are deployed to communicate meaning clearly and develop a line of thought which is sustainedly relevant to purpose; spelling, grammar and punctuation are sufficiently accurate.

   *The term "text" encompasses printed, audio or film/video text(s) which may be literary (fiction or non-fiction) or may relate to aspects of media or language.

2. **Confirming Technical Accuracy**

   An essay which does not satisfy the requirement for "sufficient" technical accuracy cannot pass. If, however, technical accuracy is deemed "sufficient", then there are no penalties or deductions for such errors.

   The definition of "sufficiently accurate" is the same as that given below for "consistently accurate", but with an allowance made for examination conditions, ie time pressure and no opportunity to redraft.

   Consistently accurate (in line with Core Skills statement)

   Few errors will be present. Paragraphs, sentences and punctuation are accurate and organised so that the writing can be clearly and readily understood. Spelling errors (particularly of high frequency words) are infrequent.

3. **Assigning a Category and Mark**

   Each essay should then be assigned to the appropriate Category as outlined in the Broad Descriptors, supported by reference to the Detailed Descriptors.

   (a) **Broad Descriptors**

   Essays which **pass** (ie meet the minimum requirements of the Performance Criteria) should be assigned to one of four categories as follows:

Category	Mark(s)	Broad descriptor
I	25	Outstanding
II	21 **or** 23	Very sound
III	17 **or** 19	Comfortably achieves the Performance Criteria
IV	13 **or** 15	Just succeeds in achieving the Performance Criteria

Essays which **fail** to meet the minimum requirements of one or more than one Performance Criterion should be assigned to one of two categories as follows:

Category	Mark(s)	Broad descriptor
V	11 **or** 9	Fails to achieve one or more than one Performance Criterion and/or to achieve sufficient technical accuracy, or is simply too thin
VI*	7 **or** 5**	Serious shortcomings

In Categories II – VI, the choice of which mark to award should be determined by the level of certainty with which the response has been assigned to the Category.

*   Essays in this Category will be extremely rare. It should be used only in cases of significant misunderstanding of a text, extreme thinness, or serious weaknesses in expression and/or technical accuracy.

** Marks below 5 could, in exceptional circumstances, be awarded – for example to a response which was of extreme brevity, perhaps just a few lines.

(b) **Detailed descriptors**

Category I (25 marks): A sophisticated response which, allowing for the pressures of examination conditions and the limited time available, is outstanding in nearly every respect. Knowledge and understanding of the text(s) are sound. The question is addressed fully and convincingly in such a way as to show insight into the text(s) as a whole, and selection of evidence to support the argument is extensive and skilful. The essay is effectively structured as a genuine response to the question. As appropriate to the task and the text(s), the candidate demonstrates a sophisticated awareness of the literary and/or linguistic techniques being exploited. There is a committed evaluative stance with respect to the text(s) and the task, although this is not necessarily explicit. Expression is controlled and fluent.

Dealing with longer texts, the response ranges effectively over the whole text where appropriate, selects effectively, and while focusing on the demands of the question, never loses sight of the text as a whole; dealing with shorter texts, the response uses a text which clearly allows the requirements of the question to be met fully, avoids "blanket coverage" and mechanistic, unfocused "analysis", and shows a pleasing understanding of the text as a whole.

Category II (21 or 23 marks): A very sound response which, allowing for the pressures of examination conditions and the limited time available, is secure in most respects. Knowledge and understanding of the text(s) are sound. The question is addressed fully in such a way as to show some insight into the text(s) as a whole, and selection of evidence to support the argument is extensive. The essay is soundly structured as a genuine response to the question. As appropriate to the task and the text(s), the candidate demonstrates a sound awareness of the literary and/or linguistic techniques being exploited. There is a clear evaluative stance with respect to the text(s) and the task, although this is not necessarily explicit. Expression is controlled.

Dealing with longer texts, the response ranges over the whole text where appropriate, selects sensibly, and while focusing on the demands of the question, never loses sight of the text as a whole; dealing with shorter texts, the response uses a text which clearly allows the requirements of the question to be met, avoids "blanket coverage" and mechanistic, unfocused "analysis", and shows a sound understanding of the text as a whole.

Category III (17 or 19 marks): A response which, allowing for the pressures of examination conditions and the limited time available, is secure in a number of respects. Knowledge and understanding of the text(s) are on the whole sound. The question is addressed adequately in such a way as to show understanding of the text as a whole, and selection of evidence to support the argument is appropriate to the task. The essay is structured in such a way as to meet the requirements of the question. As appropriate to the task and the text(s), the candidate shows an awareness of the literary and/or linguistic techniques being exploited. There is some evaluative stance with respect to the text(s) and the task, although this is not necessarily explicit. Expression is satisfactory.

Dealing with longer texts, the response makes some attempt to range over the whole text where appropriate, makes some selection of relevant evidence, and while focusing on the demands of the question, retains some sense of the text as a whole; dealing with shorter texts, the response uses a text which meets the requirements of the question, avoids excessive "blanket coverage" and mechanistic, unfocused "analysis", and shows an understanding of the text as a whole.

Category IV (13 or 15 marks): A response which, allowing for the pressures of examination conditions and the limited time available, just manages to meet the minimum standard to achieve the Performance Criteria. Knowledge and understanding of the text(s) are adequate. The question is addressed sufficiently in such a way as to show reasonable understanding of the text as a whole, and there is some evidence to support the argument. There is some evidence that the essay is structured in such a way as to meet the requirements of most of the question. As appropriate to the task and the text(s), the candidate shows some awareness of the literary and/or linguistic techniques being exploited. There is some evaluative stance with respect to the text(s) and the task, although this is not necessarily explicit. Expression is adequate.

Dealing with longer texts, the response retains some sense of the text as a whole; dealing with shorter texts, the response uses a text which meets the requirements of the question, avoids excessive use of mechanistic, unfocused "analysis", and shows some understanding of the text as a whole.

Category V (11 or 9 marks): A response will fall into this Category for a variety of reasons: it fails to achieve sufficient technical accuracy; or knowledge and understanding of the text are not deployed as a response relevant to the task; or any analysis attempted is undiscriminating and/or unfocused; or the answer is simply too thin.

Hey! I've done it

iBrightRED
PUBLISHING

Published by Bright Red Publishing Ltd, 6 Stafford Street, Edinburgh, EH3 7AU
Tel: 0131 220 5804, Fax: 0131 220 6710, enquiries: sales@brightredpublishing.co.uk,
www.brightredpublishing.co.uk

Official SQA answers to 978-1-84948-286-8
2008-2012